HOW TO MAKE
A HIT RECORD

Julian Colbeck

Tony Mitchell

Anaya Publishers Ltd
London

First published in Great Britain in 1989
by Anaya Publishers Ltd, 49 Neal Street, London WC2H 9PJ

Designer Peter Ward

British Library Cataloguing in Publication Data
is available on request

ISBN 1-85470-007-3

Typeset by Keyspools Ltd, Warrington
Printed and bound in Great Britain by
Butler & Tanner Ltd, Frome.

The Publishers would like to thank Yamaha
for their help in the preparation of this book.

CONTENTS

INTRODUCTION

●◆●◆●◆ *You've got to be kidding. If you really knew how to make a hit record you wouldn't bother telling us now, would you?*

YOU'RE probably right. And anyway, what makes a hit record in pure musical terms changes from year to year. Well, sometimes it does.

But hit records – and, to clarify our terms, we're essentially talking hit singles – are more than a brilliant voice, or a dance craze, or a sex symbol.

Or are they?

Hit records become hit records through a combination of factors; each, in isolation, being unlikely to dent the national psyche to any great degree. Put crudely, a gorgeous 15-year-old bimbette dressed, however, like one of the Bisto Kids and singing an old jazz standard recorded on *Opportunity Knocks*, will be hard pushed to make it. Pour her into a rubber mini and hand her over to Stock Aitken Waterman, however, and you're home and dry.

Which is where this book comes in. If you want alternatives to the rubber mini and SAW, it acts as a source of information on all the component parts of hitmaking. How you put them together is up to you.

We make no excuse for the fact that large chunks of this book are taken up with gear of one sort or another – instruments, recording equipment and the like.

That's how music is today, folks. No use pretendin' t'aint. Apart from anything else, it explains how so many DJs and producers are busy having hits these days and so many 'musicians' are stuck on the pub circuit.

We've got to redefine the word 'musician'. In the past, pop musicians may not always have been able to play their instruments too well but at least they bothered miming to them. And at least *someone*, somewhere had played the necessary parts.

Today, now that most of our lives have become computerised, the pretence isn't there any more. Everyone 'knows' about drum machines, everyone 'knows' about synths and computers.

Do they, indeed? What do they know? Do drum machines magically program themselves, do synths and sequencers suddenly start playing catchy little riffs?

Musicality comes from the brain, not the fingers. Beethoven was, in all probability, a lousy oboe player (he was a pretty terrible pianist by the end, too). But does that mean he was cheating because someone else played oboe parts he'd written out?

So why should someone who programs a drum machine, or inputs entire scores on a sequencer be, of necessity, unmusical? If they are, it'll show. Unmusical crud in, unmusical crud out.

There again, one man's unmusical crud is another's holiday song in Ibiza or whatever. Pop has rarely dallied with academia anyhow. It isn't supposed to.

How To Make A Hit Record deals with life and music as it is, not as the national and music press think it is nor as bitter and twisted old musicians think it should be.

Or, come to that, feminists. We don't endorse sexism in music or any other walk of life, but to pretend that the music business is anything other than male-dominated is to deceive oneself to no useful purpose. But while that may mean jobs for the boys, it has also meant plenty of hits for the girls.

Yet re-reading the book reveals one glaring omission from the list of 'essential' hitmaking ingredients, and it's called grit.

If you're not prepared to walk that extra mile, get that photo just right, phone up that last DJ, whatever it takes, then someone else probably is. And *they'll* have the hit. The only way you *won't* have a hit record is to give up. Those who battle on invariably do, and then have to sit by as they're dismissed as overnight successes!

So read, combine what you learn into a cohesive package that you can live with, and that applies to your music, and then tunnel-vision your way into the charts.

ACKNOWLEDGMENTS

Wittingly or unwittingly, the following people have helped the authors to arrive at the opinions and conclusions presented in this book: Dave Bedford, Brian Bonnar, Elvina, Jeremy Lascelles, Lizann Peppard, Dafydd Rees, David Seville, Pete Smith.

SONGWRITING

●▶●▶●▶ *10 per cent inspiration, 90 per cent perspiration*

ASK ANY popster, producer, record company exec, publisher, or DJ what's the single most important ingredient of a hit record, and nine out of ten will say it's the song.

The thing is, do you need to write it? Must you be a songwriter in order to have a hit or to get a record deal?

The answer, as it happens, is no.

If you look at the whole history of hit singles, songwriting performers are almost rare; it's only recently that the line between performer and songwriter (traditionally removed only once every ten years as the latest singer-songwriter fad sweeps in) has blurred beyond distinction.

However, although you do not *need* to write your own material, it has to be said that songwriting ability is a definite plus.

Not only do record companies get far more excited about people they can think of as creative 'artists' but you yourself will have more control over your career. If successful, you'll also be considerably richer thanks to the flood of additional money you'll be earning from record sales, publishing agreements, and radio/TV play.

Incredibly, even if you're not successful, you can earn good money out of songwriting thanks to the absurd situation whereby the writer of a single's B-side gets the same money from the sale of the record as the writer of the A-side!

The art of
songwriting

If the song really 'works', ie no matter how it's performed it still sounds okay, then all other considerations, from production to promotion, can be viewed in a different light. In a way, such considerations then assume the role of *adding to* a record's success, as opposed to creating that success in the first place.

Conversely, a duff song is going to need heavyweight help along the way if it's to make it. And even then money doesn't automatically buy a hit.

Tracy Chapman is one of the few recent artists whose success came on a singer-songwriter ticket.

Songwriting is both art and craft. Ten per cent inspiration, 90 per cent perspiration, as one sage put it. And, not surprisingly, the best way to improve your songwriting is to stick at it. The more you write the better you'll get.

This may sound obvious but it's amazing how many people put off writing that hit because they're waiting for some blinding flash of inspiration. If you can get into the habit of finishing songs – no matter how second rate or clichéd you might think them at the time – then a) you'll improve, and b) you stand a chance of writing that hit.

The music

Every songwriter has his own trick or system for writing songs. Some start with a melody in their head, others just noodle about on piano or guitar until a chord sequence starts to sound catchy; some people like refining a band jam into a song. No one way is any better than another. If it works for you, great. Stick with it.

But however tricky it is to start talking about a 'good' song, if you study successful records, you'll discover that there are certain common denominators which, if you're after a hit, are worth examining.

1. Melody

Lead vocal, the tune, call it what you like but it's still the most important part of a song. The tune is what people whistle on their way to the record store, not the bass drum pattern or the virtuosity of the string part.

Although it's easy to spot a catchy tune (it's catchy, you keep singing it, that's how!), precisely what makes it catchy is another matter. There's no magic number of notes, no specific intervals, involved.

All one can say is PAY ATTENTION TO THE LEAD LINE. When you're in the process of writing sing your proposed tune to yourself, by itself. Does it stand up? Can you remember it the next day? (An excellent test: if you can't, how do you expect anyone else to?)

Traps to avoid include sticking religiously to the top note of your chord sequence, endless repetition (unless you fancy re-writing 'One Note Samba'), and boringly static rhythms, even though any singer worth his salt should be able to inject some life into too pedestrian a part.

2. Rhythm

There are very few hit records you can't dance to. It doesn't have to be an Instant Party Favourite – it might just be good to smooch to, or whatever. But if your beloved song has 18 time changes, or limps along in some kind of funereal shuffle, then, well, you're at a distinct disadvantage.

Tempo, and the 'magic' figure of 120 bpm, is dealt with on page 92, but rhythm in songwriting terms is all about consistency and feel. Consistency is relatively simple: avoid sticking bars of 5/4 in a straight ahead 4/4 song; avoid slowing down/speeding up sections – unless you're writing for the Greek wedding market.

Of course feel is a less tangible. But there are still ways to test how you're progressing. Can *you* dance to it? Can your partner dance to it? Play the bare bones of what you have to friends and watch their reactions: yawning/sloping off to make coffee are bad signs. Foot tapping, nodding, smiling, is what you're after.

3. The Hook

There are many definitions of what constitutes a hook, but, as the word implies, a hook is something that 'hooks' you in, makes you want to listen again, makes you want to buy. It can be a catchy vocal line; it can be a catchy instrumental line (*that* sax part on Gerry Rafferty's 'Baker Street', *that* piano part on Bruce Hornsby's 'The Way It Is'). It can be the entire chorus, or it can be a single word.

If you'll forgive the expression, getting too hung up on the hook is a waste of time. As often as not, the hook is what turns a bunch of old noodled chords into the beginnings of a song, or a mindless hum into a melody. In other words, it is often precisely that which inspires you to continue the work in the first place.

While it's true that most hit songs do have a hook of some description, leave the labelling of which particular bit of your song constitutes the hook to the DJs and musicologists. If you just concentrate on what sounds and feels good, the chances are your hook will be generated naturally. If, when it comes to recording, your song appears 'hookless', and desparately in need of one, the necessary part(s) can be added at that stage (see page 54).

Sometimes a song – and invariably a great song – can almost write itself. Great songwriters such as (like him or not) Paul McCartney have often talked about how some songs seem to reveal themselves – as if from some kind of giant song repository in the sky! – as opposed to being 'written' as such.

Aside from putting in the hours, there are no ways you can increase the chances of this happening, and you are in fact more likely to find yourself in the opposite situation of:

Getting stuck

Those who have tried songwriting will know the problem only too well. You've come up with a great chorus but you're completely stumped for a verse. Or you've got a great verse and chorus but you need one more section. Or you just cannot find a strong enough tune for the verse. There are many fun-packed ways of getting stuck alright, and here are just a few possible solvents:

- ● ● ● ● ● ● ● ➤ Change key. Either change key in the middle of your song, or play what you have (the verse, the chorus) in another key. Keys have different characters and sometimes the different slant another key may put on your work will be enough to inspire you out of trouble.

- ● ● ● ● ● ● ● ➤ If you're not already doing so, set up a drum machine pattern which will encourage you to keep going. If you're already doing this, change pattern, even if it's temporarily not the pattern/feel you had in mind.

● ● ● ● ● ● ➧ Substitute chords. Use chords which share a common ground: instead of going back to C Major every time, go back to A Minor, or A Minor 7th, or E Minor etc.

● ● ● ● ● ● ➧ Minor to Major. Don't be afraid to have a Minor key verse after a Major key chorus.

● ● ● ● ● ● ➧ Mix and Match. The Beatles' 'A Day In The Life' is a mix of a Lennon song (the beginning) and a McCartney one ('Woke up.' etc). Plenty of people do this, either between songs (or bits of songs) of their own, or of their partner's. Sometimes you may need to alter the key to fit; sometimes, off the wall though it might be in theory, it works as it is.

Classic song hooks are usually, but not always, vocal. With his '70s hit 'Baker Street', Gerry Rafferty created a song that owed its catchiness primarily to a memorable sax line.

How to write songs if you don't play an instrument

This used to be far more difficult than it is today. Now there are a number of solutions, aside from the obvious one of working in conjunction with someone who does play.

● Get help in the shape of a good quality home keyboard (see page 61); an instrument that can generate accompaniment patterns and such with no manual or instrumental skill required – just a pair of ears!

● Work with personal computer recording software (see page 57). You'll need to be more technically (not musically) inclined than for the above, but the computer and linked-up instrument modules can do the playing provided you tell them (loosely) what to do.

● Drum machines. You don't need to be Steve Gadd, nor Einstein, to press 'Start' on a drum machine. Armed with such and a cassette recorder, write using drum patterns and a vocal line. Then, go for the obvious:

● Find a partner or an arranger who can work with you to develop your ideas into recordable songs.

Lyrics

The difference between a lyric and poem, according to legendary American lyricist Sammy Cahn, is that a poem is meant 'for the eye' and a lyric 'for the ear'. Since their work appeals to different senses, it's not surprising, then, that a good poet or indeed writer of prose can still make a useless lyricist.

Some people simply have the knack of lyric writing. And if they analysed how or why they did what they did, they'd probably dry up. So they don't. Fine. Mere mortals, meanwhile, have to soldier on as best they can.

What makes a great lyric? Are lyrics important? Can you learn how to write lyrics. Yes to all three! A great lyric is one that helps a song to become a hit. The reasons *why* it helped the song become a hit is another matter: it could be thought-provoking as in a protest song; it could be plain funny like Squeeze's 'Up The Junction'; it could touch a nerve as does Mike & The Mechanics' 'The Living Years'.

What is important is that the lyrics fit the music. If Kylie Minogue starts prattling on about ecology in a breezy, dancey, up-tempo setting, it's probably not going to work – sugar-with-the-spice subtlety hardly being pop's strongest feature.

It's also important that lyrics fit the music in a literal sense. Lyrics that demand

Right: Every now and then, the line between performance and songwriting blurs. Howard Jones is one of few recent artists whose success came on a singer-songwriter-keyboard-player ticket.

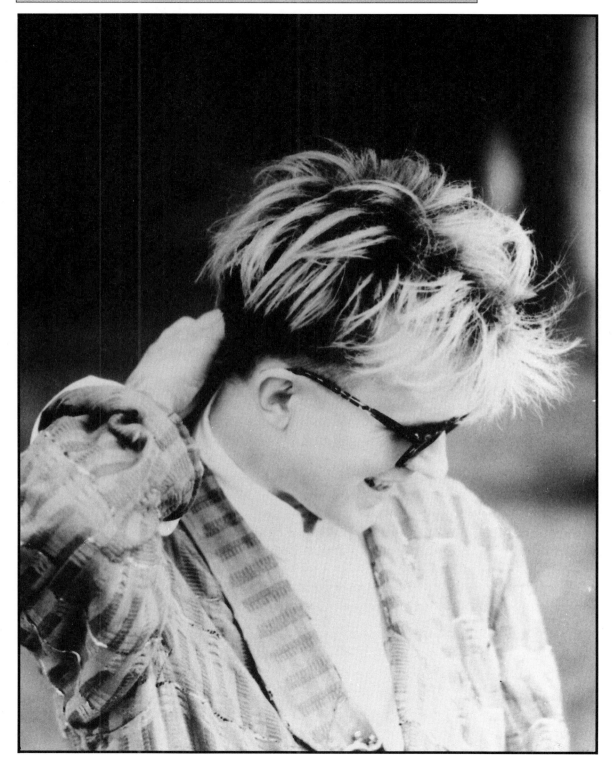

a singer goes 'I-I-I-I fee-ee-eel so happee-ee-ee' rarely get beyond the drawing board.

In answer to the second question – are lyrics important *anyway*? – they're only unimportant if you have other compensating factors like the music's dynamite, or you're a 16-year-old female with a 38-inch chest, you're an established star who can get away with anything, or you're only producing 'mindless' dance music anyway, etc.

But even if your songs do fit into one of these categories, a good lyric ain't going to *hurt*, so why limit yourself?

Okay, so I won't. Now what?

First of all, be prepared to put in some effort. Most good lyrics have been honed and refined into their final form. Don't just stick with the first lines to enter your head. Like it or not, 50 per cent of a song's earning power comes from the lyrics, so earn that money.

Apart from those already mentioned there are no golden rules about pop lyrics. They don't *have* to scan, they don't *have* to mean anything, they don't *have* to flow, they don't even *have* to be memorable – aside from, preferably, the title. Whenever one does stumble upon such attributes, mind you, do they ever make a difference!

On the other hand, a lyric's most damning crime is to sound dull. Words like 'just' and 'really' and 'seems' are OUT in all but otherwise exceptionally brilliant settings. So too are interminable drivellings about 'feeling' this and that, and 'needing' something or someone, particularly if one is 'needing' it or them 'so bad'.

If you want to make a go of lyric writing, you have two basic choices in terms of approach: the 'something to say and finding an interesting/different/neat way of saying it – but using plain English – approach', or what is best termed the 'colourful guff' approach, ie it sounds wonderful but means, to all but the odd weed-enfeebled, trendy Harvard English professor, nothing whatsoever.

Either will do fine.

For the first approach you must either have plenty of things you do want to say, or else you must look for inspiration. For which you can:

● ● ● ● ● ● ● ➤ Read all the newspapers.

● ● ● ● ● ● ● ➤ Listen as opposed to talk.

● ● ● ● ● ● ● ➤ See films, go to art gallerys, read books.

● ● ● ● ● ● ● ➤ And keep a notebook.

For the second approach the sound of the words is far more important than their meaning. Phrases, well-known or otherwise, help a lot in this respect. A book of idioms, phrases, or quotations can help considerably, as can a rhyming dictionary (never mind the sense, feel the rhyme) and a Thesaurus. In fact a rhyming dictionary is an essential piece of kit.

Further inspirational tips that lyricists have been known to recommend range from studying horse-racing fixtures, to advertising slogans, booze, slang, and jargon. Again, keep a notebook and jot down unusual or colourful and evocative words.

General lyric
writing tips

Put a weak rhyme before a strong one.
- Preserve the natural emphasis of a word or phrase.
- Use imagery. Paint pictures.

- If you're telling a story in a lyric, try writing the story in prose first so that you can see where you're going, how the story develops.
- Make sure you know where a lyric is coming from. Is the singer an observer, or the person to whom something is happening? Be consistent.

If you're serious about songwriting, a four-track cassette recorder ('Portastudio') such as the Tascam Porta 05 will be an invaluable asset for developing ideas at home.

Songwriter's kit

If you're serious about songwriting you should acquire most of the following:

● ● ● ● ● ● ● ▶ Cassette recorder for jotting down notes – lyrics/concepts/music.
● ● ● ● ● ● ● ▶ Portastudio (mikes/instruments) at home for song development.
● ● ● ● ● ● ● ▶ Drum machine.
● ● ● ● ● ● ● ▶ Rhyming dictionary & Thesaurus.
● ● ● ● ● ● ● ▶ Large stock of notepads and pens.

Registering your songs

As soon as you have reduced your song to any 'material form', ie recorded it, or scored it out on manuscript paper, you have proof of copyright. In theory, that's it. You don't actually need to do anything else to register your song. But song stealing does happen, and if you're worried about it, then place a recording of your song plus a lyric sheet in an envelope, send it to yourself and don't open it. Or you may want to keep it with your lawyer, if you have one.

Contacts

British Academy of Songwriters, Composers & Authors, 34 Hanway St, London W1P 9DE (01-436-2261)
    The Society of International Songwriters & Composers, 12 Trewartha Rd, Praa Sands, Penzance. Cornwall TR20 9ST (0736-762826)
    The Musicians Union, 60-62 Clapham Rd, London SW9 OJJ (01-582-5566)

Song contests

The problem with music contests is that although winning is touted as being a kind of passport to fame and fortune such an eventuality is very rare indeed. Some would go further and argue that song/band contests are the kiss of death. But whatever else they may or may not be, song contests do encourage people to write songs. And you can make reasonable money from them as well.

Books

Songwriter's Guide to Collaboration, Walter Carter (Omnibus)

The Craft of Lyric Writing, Sheila Davis (Omnibus)

Successful Lyric Writing, Sheila Davis (Omnibus)

The Songwriter's Rhyming Dictionary, Sammy Cahn (Souvenir Press)

Walker's Rhyming Dictionary of the English Language (RKP Ltd)

LEARNING
AN INSTRUMENT

•▶•▶•▶ *Technical prowess does not a million make*

'Difficult?' asked Dr Samuel Johnson, upon suffering a violinist's 'virtuoso' performance one evening, 'I wish it were impossible.'

J OHNSON'S remark (made, incidentally, in the eighteenth century!) seems particularly pertinent when you hear endless techno-soloing on instrument demos or 'serious' fusion records. And the sad fact is that technical prowess on a musical instrument does not necessarily equal a hit record. At times it can even be a disadvantage.

Although becoming a virtuoso is unlikely to increase your chances of a hit, learning an instrument to at least a reasonable standard does help your cause. Not only will it improve your ability to write songs, but it'll allow you to demo them yourself, perhaps master them, and finally promote them.

'Yes,' you say, 'but I've left it too late. It'll take too long. It's too difficult. It's no fun.'

Wrong, wrong, wrong, wrong, wrong.

The days of hatchet-faced teachers rapping knuckles with rulers, of endless scales and arpeggios, of dreary folk songs, of tapping out military two-steps, of three years' worth of squeaks and squawks, are over.

Why? Several things, really. First, to play a pop/rock instrument never has required the technique of Paganini. Secondly, teaching methods have been brought kicking and screaming into the twentieth century with things like teaching videos, computers etc. Thirdly, many modern pop/rock instruments do not require the same level of *manual* skills as did/do classical instruments.

Learning a pop/rock instrument, to a point where it will be genuinely useful in your career, need not be a lifetime's exercise. It can even be fun. And after all you don't learn an instrument to the total exclusion of everything else. Life can go on as well.

If you want to make hit records, to make music your career, the only possible reason for not learning an instrument is because you're too damn lazy!

Which
instrument?

There's no 'best' instrument to learn. True, if you're a triangle player or a killer on the sackbutt, your chances of success might be rather slim, but of all the regular rock instruments – guitar, bass, drums, keyboards, sax – the best one for you is the one you fancy playing.

The Yamaha Disklavier – taking player-pianos into the 21st century.

Keyboards

While it's true that you don't need to be classically trained to play synths and samplers, to say that *anyone* can play keyboards without *any* ability whatsoever, is equally misleading. Learning a few chords is not difficult; getting your fingers around individual notes takes time and practice. And that's just the physical stuff. Few keyboard players survive without some knowledge and understanding of instrument technology (sequencing, sampling, programming, MIDI).

Guitar

The guitar is the classic rock instrument, certainly *the instrument* to choose if you want to be out there, centre stage, posing. Learning to play chords and the odd riff should not take long – months as opposed to years – and because at least part of its attraction is that it's a very human sounding instrument, it is possible to turn limited technique into a style. Although some people learn bass right from the word go, most move on to bass having first grasped the basics of guitar.

Drums

Some would have you believe that the drummer's days are numbered. For a variety of reasons (among which are the sound, feel, and look of 'real' drums), this is very doubtful. Although the basic requirements of a good sense of rhythm, co-ordination and stamina remain, advances in drum technology require the modern player to be equally capable of programming drum machines and even using samplers (see page 54).

Brass

There's always room for a good brass player, as a first or second instrument (many keyboard players double on sax). But brass instruments tend to be instruments you can't bluff on. Time has to be put in. Being monophonic, brass instruments are not ideal for use in songwriting; nor, unless you become another Kenny G or Grover Washington Jr, for getting you a hit record.

Self teaching or lessons?

Put it this way: lessons never hurt anybody. And they'll make you practise because you don't want to waste your money. A few lessons can save you a lot of time in the long run too and, if nothing else, they'll give you something to reject later on. Many professionals continue to go back for the odd lesson throughout their career (Journey's highly accomplished singer Steve Perry being a well-known case in point) just to keep them in trim.

Although you'll probably find your local education institute runs guitar or keyboard evening classes, the chances of such a grounding having any bearing

on your ability to make a hit record is highly remote. For that, you'll need private lessons, preferably from a professional in your field (if you want to be a country music star, lessons from your local Def Leppard clone are unlikely to help).

Don't be afraid to try several teachers until you find the right person for you. Signing up for a year's worth of lessons 'sight unseen' is probably a bad idea.

Costs

Good lessons costing less than £10 per hour will be hard to find. Broadly speaking you get what you pay for – as with most things. Cheap lessons, if the tuition is cut rate also, are useless.

Books

In isolation, an instructional book is the hardest system to use. Look at it sensibly: music is an aural medium; pop is both aural and visual. Books are fine

Many guitarists are self-taught, but most professional drummers say there's no substitute for lessons from a drum teacher. Drum clinics like this also encourage development of technique.

as back-up, giving you exercises, the odd tip etc, but the best way to learn an instrument is to listen to, see, and learn from someone who already knows.

Cassettes

Until teaching videos came onto the market, cassettes were the best value aids, and they're still well worth investigating.

Videos

A medium that lets you see as well as hear how to play an instrument has to be the next best thing to your own private tutor. Be warned, however, that many are cashing in on the genre, and some videos can be little more than promotional items for the 'star' player concerned, which is fine for entertainment but useless for teaching you how to play.

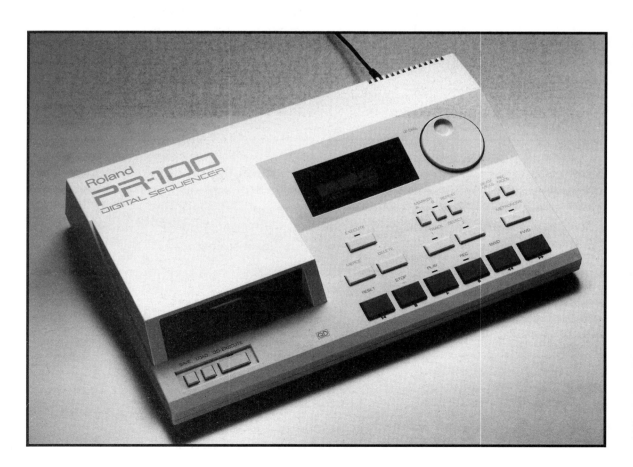

Software

Teaching software for certain instruments/pieces of equipment is a progressive and, because you can interact, stimulating way to learn, well, keyboards primarily.

Two companies lead the field: Roland, with ISM (Intelligent System of Music), and Yamaha, with special software for its Disklavier (MIDI-based player piano) instruments.

ISM is a system that uses a Roland digital piano, the MT-32 instrument module, and the PR-100 sequencer. Special sequencer disks enable you to learn in a live music setting, with accompaniments you can control in terms of speed, keys, left hand/right hand, on/off etc. Although most disks are prepared for keyboard players, some are available with accompaniments suited to other instruments.

The Yamaha Disklavier approach is less flexible but you have the advantages of using what is effectively (also) a real acoustic piano, and being actually able to see notes being 'played' by the player piano mechanism. A large library of songs, both classical and pop, is available on disks which you load into the Disklavier itself.

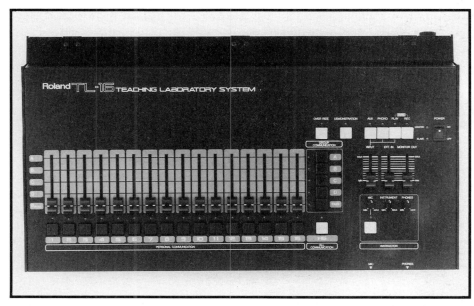

Left: Another electronic teaching aid is this PR-100 sequencer which, as part of Roland's ISM (Intelligent System of Music) concept, allows you to learn at home with realistic accompaniments.

Above: Japanese instrument companies like Roland and Yamaha are very education-orientated. This TL-16 'mother unit' is part of Roland's Teaching Laboratory System for music schools.

Vocals

If the song is the most important ingredient when it comes to making a hit record, the lead vocal is the most important ingredient in the song.

Singing is all too often taken for granted in rock. Many people think they can either sing or they can't. They don't think of the voice as an instrument – something that can be learned, used properly or abused, needs maintenance etc.

Most rock singers would like you to believe that their voice is natural (whatever *that* means). Lessons and exercises and warming up don't really go with the image. Of course many singers do 'just sing', and constantly abuse their instrument with booze, late nights and no technique. They're normally the ones who end up with nodules. It all depends upon how many hits you're planning on having I guess.

Established singers may find it difficult to backtrack and learn how to breathe properly. But if you're starting out, as a lead or even backing vocalist, tuition now may save you untold grief later on.

- Learning a wind instrument is often recommended as a way of improving your breathing and your pitching.
- Avoid drinking milk before singing – it's even worse than booze!
- Keep in shape. Although you should think of your voice as an instrument, it is still one that's permanently attached to your body.
- Remember: you can't buy another voice when yours packs up.

Books

GUITAR
Beginning Rock Guitar, Artie Traum (Amsco)
Rock 'n' Roll Guitar Case Chord Book, Russ Shipton (Wise publications)
The Complete Rock & Pop Guitar Player, Mick Barker, Rick Cardinali & Roger Day (Wise publications)
Instant Guitar: Play Today (Wise publications)
Advanced Picture Chords For Guitar, Russ Shipton (Wise publications)
Play Rock Guitar, Mike Clifford (Amsco)

DRUMS
How To Play Drums, James Blades and Johnny Dean (Elm Tree)
The Complete Drum Tutor, Lloyd Ryan
The Complete Electronic Percussion Book, Dave Crombie (Amsco)

KEYBOARDS
Play Rock Keyboards, Dewi Evans (Amsco)
The Keyboardist's Picture Chord Encyclopedia, Leonard Vogler (Wise)
How to Play Electronic Keyboards, Mike Beecher & Rosalyn Asher (Elm Tree)
Synthesizer Technique, the editors of *Keyboard* magazine (Hal Leonard)

BRASS
The Complete Saxophone Player: Omnibus Edition, Raphael Ravenscroft (Wise)
How To Play Trumpet, Digby Fairweather (Elm Tree)

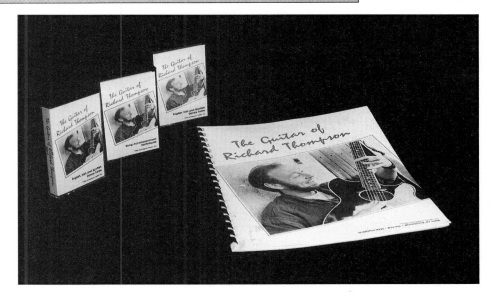

They'll never match private tuition, but tutors – especially from cult figures like Richard Thompson – can inspire and instruct to good effect.

Cassettes

GUITARS
Hot Licks (all styles inc. bass)
Star Styles (bass licks, Beck, Blackmore, Clapton, Yngwie Malmsteen, Page, Rhoads and more)
Star Guitar (bass, country, blues rock, hard rock,metal)

Star Licks Master Series (Earl Greco, Hendrix, Albert Lee, Steve Lukather, Larry Carlton, Ray Flacke and more)

KEYBOARDS
The Rock Piano Tapes, Simon McCheane (Satellite)
Hot Licks (piano & synth)

Videos

GUITARS
Hot Licks (Arlen Roth [several styles], Vinnie Moore, Joe Pass, William Kannengiser, John Entwistle, Stuart Hamm)
Star Licks (Steve Lukather, Larry Carlton, Brian May, Albert Lee, Al McKay, Jeff Watson, Michael Angelo, Rick Emmett, Chet Atkins, Brothers Johnson, Jeff Berlin)
DCI Videos (Adrian Belew, John Scofield, Jaco Pastorius)
Rumark Video (Barney Kessel)

BRASS
Hot Licks (Steve Pocaro, Bruce Lowe)

DRUMS
Hot Licks (Drum Master Class, Tommy Aldridge)
DCI Videos (Steve Gadd, Louie Bellson, Ed Thigpen, Max Roach, Bill Bruford, Steve Smith, Kenny Aronoff)
Star Licks (Chet McCraken)

KEYBOARDS
DCI Videos (Richard Tee, Chick Corea, George Duke)
Star Licks (Steve Pocaro, Bruce Lowe)

GUITARS

• ◆ • ◆ • ◆   *The bedrock instruments of rock and pop*

DESPITE the undeniable prominence of computer-based instruments and equipment in the production of contemporary chart music, the guitar remains the bedrock instrument of rock and pop music.

It's great for writing songs on, can be used to create sounds which we still find fresh and inspiring after nearly 40 years of rock and roll, can be turned, in the hands of a gifted player, into an excitingly dynamic, expressive solo instrument. and remains undoubtedly the most potent vehicle for posing with on stage or in front of the cameras!

Even when it is not apparently present at all on a record, or there only in a heavily processed form – even sampled and played back by keyboard players – its spiritual influence is still very strong, as the very structure of pop music still seems inextricably linked to the note and chord progressions most readily created on the guitar.

Its value as a compositional tool matches or exceeds that of the piano, and it's still about the cheapest way of making satisfying musical noises.

The instruments

Admittedly, the kind of instrument you buy and the way you approach playing will be conditioned to an extent by your ambitions. For most aspiring players, there is only one choice: the electric guitar. For any number of obvious reasons, it's the most popular, and there are various different sub-types of electric guitar to consider.

The vast majority of electric guitars you'll find in any store today are six-string solid body instruments, because this is the essential rock 'n' roll axe. The Fender Stratocaster and Gibson Les Paul are archetypal solid guitars whose designs date from the early 1950s and are much-copied today.

There are also semi-acoustic (sometimes called semi-solid) guitars, which come either in thin-bodied or fat-bodied styles, typified respectively by the Gibson ES-335 and Switchmaster. All such instruments are fitted with steel strings and electromagnetic pickups.

Various types of electrified acoustic instrument are also available, and in recent years these electro-acoustic designs, usually fitted with piezo-electric pick-ups buried in the bridge, have been joined by a new type of piezo-equipped instrument, the 'solid classic', which looks like a Spanish guitar even down to its nylon strings, but has a solid body.

Pure acoustic guitar sounds are also currently fashionable on hit records; these instruments come basically in folk (steel-strung) or classical (nylon/bronze-strung Spanish) guise.

Fashion has also revived the pleasingly melodic, full-bodied jingle-jangle sound of the 12-string guitar in its acoustic, semi-acoustic and solid forms.

The Fender Stratocaster and derivative 'superstrats' have been the '80s' most prolific guitars; the whole range of Strats and other Fender models are displayed at Fender's London A&R Centre.

The 'superstrat'

Returning to the archetypal solid guitar, this is currently to be found most prolifically in the guise of what's called a 'superstrat'.

'Superstrat' is a generic term for any instrument based on the body shape of Fender's legendary Stratocaster but with refinements in the hardware and electronics, generally including the fitting of a bridge humbucking pick-up to boost soloing power and a locking tremolo system for 'dive-bombing'.

The superstrat is an attempt to have the best of both worlds – the world of the Stratocaster with its whining, cutting treble tones and dive-bomb engineering, and the world of the humbucking pick-up – traditionally represented by Gibson guitars like the Les Paul – with its louder, fatter, richer tonal output and better sustain qualities.

But why the Superstrat and not, say, the Superpaul? The answer is probably nine-tenths image and one tenth practicality. The Strat was Jimi Hendrix's chosen axe and is, therefore, the guitar of guitar heroes; it is also better suited tonally and expressively to today's largely digitally-created music.

Already, however, there has been much talk of a Les Paul revival. Every fad must have its backlash, and frankly it matters less now than ever that you have the right label on your axe's headstock, as long as *you're* happy with the instrument.

Choosing your weapon

What else should influence your choice? If you see yourself ultimately as *part of a team* which creates hit records, then you may decide to pursue the well-trodden road of technical virtuosity, concentrate on becoming a great soloist and hope that it leads to a gig in a successful band or to sessions for top producers. In which case you'll be looking for a guitar with the guts and character for lead work.

Then again, if you're a budding singer-songwriter you're more likely to see your instrument as an aid to writing your own hit material. In which case your ability to throw chords together and layer a vocal line over them in an interesting way is going to be far more important than great technical skill. And the guitar's overall tonal character will be more important than, say, ease of access to the 21st fret.

Bass guitar

Deciding to play bass guitar may mean that you see yourself essentially in the support role. All guitar-based rock bands still use bass players, but most records in the charts have synthesized or sampled bass lines, usually programmed on a sequencer and tied in with a drum machine.

Virtuoso bass-playing may, therefore, earn you bags of kudos and sessions, while solid dependable work may establish you as the reliable backbone to a rock group's sound. But rarely do either really put you in the frontline for action or money.

Still, if bass-playing is your chosen route to success, what do you need to know? Most guitar makers also make basses, but there have always been specialist bass companies too, and they've been responsible for some of the key developments subsequently taken on board by the big boys.

Thus, from its start in life as a basic four-string, solid, fretted version of the double bass, the last two decades have seen the bass guitar undergo a series of transformations, succesfully incorporating along the way such features as fretless fingerboards, active electronics, structural plastic bodies, graphite necks and headless tuning systems.

The current fad in basses is for five- and six-stringed instruments. These massive-necked beasts are surprisingly popular considering how difficult they are to play, but whether they will actually oust the traditional four-string format or simply co-exist with it as a minority interest remains to be seen.

In general the price bands for basses are similar to those for guitars, though you usually expect to pay more for a given quality of bass owing to higher production costs.

Acoustics and semi-acoustics

Once upon a time, everyone who played electric or bass guitar first learnt on an acoustic, but with the reasonable cost of electrics these days, this is quite unnecessary unless you plan to make acoustic guitar your real forte. Straight electrics are much easier to play.

On the other hand, if you're strapped for cash and can't immediately afford an amp and/or the transport to carry it around, acoustic guitar does represent a go anywhere, play anytime option.

Better still, an electro-acoustic or semi-acoustic gives you enough volume to play without an amp, but something that can also be plugged into an amp whenever there's one around. For electrified acoustic guitars, expect to pay as little as £50 new for something reasonably playable.

However, all the other pseudo-acoustics – jazz semis, thin semis and solid classic guitars – tend to cost considerably more than their equivalent quality solid brethren because there's more work involved and/or they're relatively small-run products.

Guitar and Bass guitar synthesisers

These have been a reality of sorts for more than a decade. But today, despite a fair amount of product choice from pioneers Roland and more recent entrants such as Shadow and Casio, these instruments are still of minority interest.

Part of the problem is cost; for even the most basic guitar synth set-up, you still have to pay much more than for just a guitar or just a synth.

But a major drawback remains in the technology; a guitar is just not a very good triggering device for electronic sounds, and attempts to make it work as one inevitably result in compromise, most noticeably in tracking accuracy (the ability of the synth to follow your fingering) and triggering speed (there's a noticeable delay when you pluck low notes).

Until guitar synths are as usable as guitars or keyboards and as cheap as FX pedals they'll probably remain a luxury/novelty for the musician who already has everything else.

Rickenbacker, one of the legendary guitar names of the '60s, is still a popular brand today with players like The Bangles' Susannah Hoffs who prize its archetypal jangly pop associations.

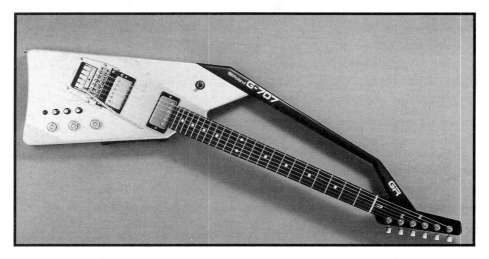

Does it look good in front of the mirror? Roland, pioneers of guitar synthesis, adopted this suitably space-age look for their current guitar synth controller, the G-707.

Buying an
electric guitar
(or bass)

If you're concerned only with getting yourself a hit record, there are just three golden rules when buying an electric guitar:

★ *Does it look good in front of the mirror?*

★ *Does it look good in front of the mirror?*

★ *Does it look good in front of the mirror?*

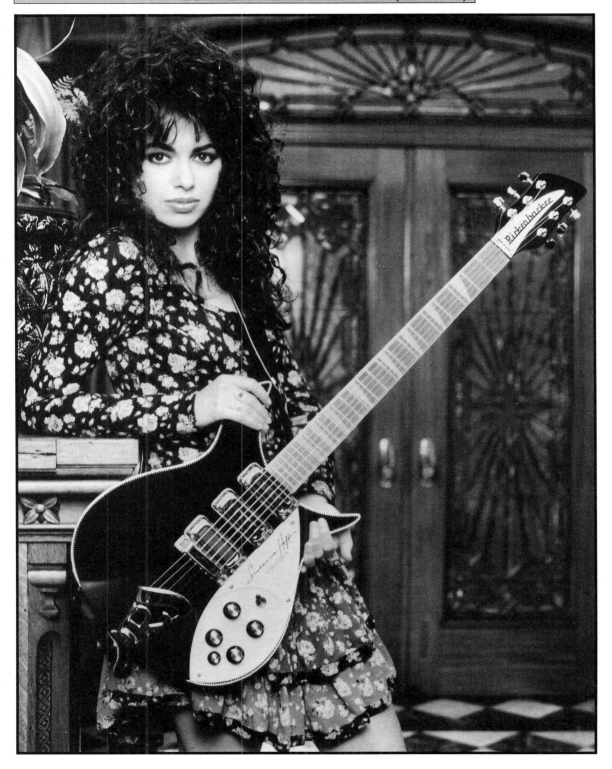

If, however, you want to have a deeper relationship with your instrument, there are a few other questions to consider:

○ Does it feel comfortable when you strap it on?

○ Does the neck just cry out to be played?

○ Can you get pleasing sounds out of it the instant it's plugged in, right there in the shop?

○ Can you carry on getting pleasing sounds out of it after half an hour of playing, or are you already bored?

○ Is it ultimately a one-sound guitar (fine, if the one sound it has is the one you want)?

And if you want to get really technical – and especially if you're parting with several hundred quid – here are some other things to check:

● The neck is not warped.

● The frets are properly finished, with no ragged ends.

● The guitar is properly set up so that strings do not 'choke' in any fret positions.

● Intonation is correct – notes or chords played around the twelfth fret sound perfectly in tune with those played up by the nut.

● When you bend individual strings, they return to proper pitch when you let them go; ditto with all six strings when you use the tremolo.

● The electronics work: all controls do something, preferably without crackles, deadspots or earth-loop hum.

How important
is the amplifier?

Like the guitar, amplification is very much a matter of personal taste. Output volume aside, rhythm players often want a range of bright, 'clean' sounds while lead players usually demand valve-type distortion to provide the requisite powerful, sustained soloing 'voice'.

Most modern amplifiers therefore cater for both needs – although 'valve' sounds will only be created by actual valves on top-priced products, since traditional valve technology is far more expensive than modern solid state technology.

When trying out a guitar to find out what sounds it is capable of, therefore, try as many different amp set-ups as possible. Sometimes, a guitar that sounds great 'clean' will sound naff on a distortion setting, or vice versa.

Try effects pedals too; an average sounding guitar can often be greatly enhanced just by chorus, though it's worth remembering that using any one effect all the time soon becomes boring, so it's better to find something that doesn't absolutely need effects to make it sound okay.

And remember – the greater the variety of instrument types you try within your price-range, the better. You might go hunting for a superstrat and find you actually feel far more comfortable with a jumbo semi-acoustic.

Instrument
sources

The electric guitars and basses most of us buy today are made in the Far East. Japan, once the main source of mid-priced instruments of decent quality, now tends to manufacture mostly upmarket product, and has been replaced in the middle-market by Korea.

The real budget-priced instruments tend to come currently from Taiwan, though other cheap sources like Indonesia and India are coming on stream.

America, traditional home of the electric guitar but ousted from its pre-eminent position by soaring manufacturing costs, tends to produce upmarket, custom-built instruments these days, while some American brand names have been preserved by partnerships with Japanese or Korean manufacturers, with guitars being designed in the States but manufactured elsewhere.

Britain and other European countries all have indigenous guitar-makers producing good mid-to-high priced instruments, though not on a scale comparable with the Orient.

Costs

Playable electrics start at well under **£100**. The bodies will be plywood or some other woody composite, not solid timber, they'll have a basic tremolo unit (if at all), fairly mediocre pick-ups and a limited tonal range. But they'll do the job.

Between **£100** and **£200**, you can move up the scale towards better-made Korean product and expect, at the top of the bracket, quite impressive overall construction/fittings/finish quality.

£200–300 buys you top quality Korean with genuine timber bodies and also gets you into the low-end British and Japanese bracket. Better pick-ups, better woods, better overall finishing can make an appreciable difference here.

£300–500 gives you access to the vast, well made, well useable mid-range product from Britain and Japan plus the cheapest US product.

£500–800 brings you top-of-the range British and Japanese instruments as well as low-mid-priced US-originated product, using traditional top-grade guitar woods.

£800 and above gets you well into the American market and the rarified atmosphere of handbuilt instruments in which all kinds of exotic woods and luxury fittings are the order of the day.

Buying secondhand

This is a very good way of getting better quality than you could afford new.

Apply the same tests as you'd apply to a new instrument and remember that a few dents and scratches or a bit of worn plating won't affect the performance of the instrument, while the guitar's overall playability will probably have actually benefited from its being 'worn in' by a previous owner.

There are plenty of private secondhand bargains to be found in the music press, while most music stores have some traded-in stock along with the new stuff on the walls.

Who's who – a guide to the major guitar manufacturers

There are many, many brands of guitar on the market, and many of them are produced in the Orient by the same few factories.

The following breakdown of guitar brands concentrates on those widely available in Britain, or otherwise significant. Distributor information is included, as are briefer mentions for lesser known products.

Aria Famous ground-breaking Japanese brand largely responsible for opening up the UK market to good quality, low priced Japanese copies and original designs in the late '70s. As with other Japanese manufacturers, ground has been lost due to rising costs. Marketed today by Aria UK, the range still offers quality and value but lacks its earlier edge. Prices: mid.

Axe Mail order-only company offering unbeatable bargains for the student guitarist or bass player. Axe guitar and bass packages include strap, bag, lead, tutor books and tapes plus amplifier, both for well under £100. UK distributor: Axe. Prices: low.

Casio Casio a guitar maker? Yes, since the introduction of its 'fun' plastic guitar synths and its professional PG range of digital guitars. The PGs are basic Strat-shaped instruments with onboard digital sounds which can be played in tandem with the regular guitar sound. Additional digital sounds can be accessed by plugging in voice cards. Reviewers rate them more user-friendly than other guitar synths. Prices: high (for a guitar).

Charvel Along with Jackson, one of the real success stories of the '80s. Both ranges are produced by the American IMC company; Jacksons are the expensive, handbuilt-in-the-USA models, Charvels their designed-in-the-USA, built-in-Japan cousins. Both share superstrat configurations and are joint originators of the much-copied, but latterly protected-by-patent, pointy headstock look. Latest development is a third, low price range called Charvette. UK distributor: John Hornby

Skewes. Prices: Charvette low, Charvel mid to high, Jackson high to sky.

Encore Own-brand name of major British distributor John Hornby Skewes (alias JHS), Encore guitars occupy the important cheap and cheerful slot where low price and modest quality yield high unit sales. Prices: low.

Epiphone *See* Gibson

ESP Japanese parts company which started manufacturing whole guitars as well. Interesting for its customising potential. UK distributor: Seven Dials International. Prices: mid to high.

Fender The originators, along with Gibson, of the rock guitar and still one of the big names today owing to split US and Far Eastern production, making their own oriental copies at all levels, under the Fender Japan, Squier and lately Sunn brands. Slow at first to jump on the superstrat bandwagon – ironically as they're the producers of the one and only true Stratocaster – Fender have now caught up with fashion as well as producing updated or faithful-to-the-original versions of most of their classics. UK distributor: Arbiter. Prices: Sunn low; Squier low to mid; Fender Japan mid to high; Fender USA high to sky.

Fernandes Japanese manufacturer of high quality replicas of vintage Fender and Gibson guitars, also producing a number of original designs and superstrat-type instruments. UK distributor: PBT. Prices: mid to high.

Frontline Brand of extremely cheap, good quality Strat clones and suchlike. UK distributor: Strings & Things. Prices: low.

Gibson Along with Fender, one of the guitar greats, sadly somewhat low-profile these days owing to prices that are hard to justify and an image diluted by successive changes in ownership and manufacturing policy. In tandem with producing innumerable classic instruments, Gibson also maintains its budget brand Epiphone, consisting of pared-back versions of Gibson designs, produced first in America and later in the Far East and currently made in Korea under the Epiphone by Gibson imprint. UK distributor: Rosetti. Prices: Gibson high to sky, Epiphone low to mid.

Hohner Once lightweights of the guitar world, Hohner have come on in leaps and bounds in the last couple of years with their Professional range. These instruments represent the best Korean quality, further enhanced by EMG and Steinberger licensed fittings. As a result, Hohner's headless basses are the best cheap copies around (and 'official', too) and their guitars take some beating. There's also a cheaper range from the same distributor under the Arbor brand name. Prices: Hohner low to mid; Arbor low.

Hondo Budget range from Jackson/Charvel producers IMC, Hondo have long been a bottom-end stalwart, offering modest quality at good prices. UK distributor: John Hornby Skewes. Prices: low.

Ibanez Once the only Japanese copyists of any note, Ibanez began introducing original designs in the '70s and their stature grew as Japanese products in general became more acceptable. The company even followed Roland into the guitar synth market. By the mid-80s, high production costs had weakened the brand's position in the UK market but it has recently been relaunched – as an upmarket product endorsed by the likes of Steve Vai – by new distributors Cougar Audio. Prices: mid to high.

Jackson *See* Charvel

Kay Low priced electrics and acoustics distributed by Hohner.

The Hohner Jack is the latest in a very successful line of low-to-mid-priced Korean-made headless guitars, whose design is licensed from Steinberger.

Peavey Known primarily as a vastly successful amplification manufacturer, Peavey also produces a substantial range of guitars and basses, from cheap beginners' items through to professional 'endorsee' models like its Signature series. Quality control is assured by extensive automation, which is also a key reason why Peavey can make all-American instruments at prices that compete head on with Korean, British and low-end Japanese prices. UK Distributor: Peavey UK. Prices: low to high.

Rickenbacker This famous American maker retains the cult status that it acquired in the '60s with artists like The Beatles, The Who and The Byrds, and survives today despite high unit manufacturing costs by concentrating on numerous special editions that complement its standard range. Distinctive looks and a distinctive sound have been maintained against all competition. UK distributor: Rickenbacker International UK. Prices: high to sky.

Roland Pioneers of guitar synthesis, Roland have been perfecting the electronic guitar for well over a decade. From early, limited analogue systems, the company went on to introduce the hex guitar pick-up which is now a standard element of most guitar synth designs, and apply it to the control of a succession of increasingly sophisticated six-voice synths, up to the current range of MIDI-based products, with digital signal processing waiting in the wings for the next generation. UK distributor: Roland UK. Prices (for complete systems): high.

Marlin Another low cost brand from Hohner.

Maya Cheap and cheerful oriental line from Stentor, noted for its baby-sized electrics. Prices: low.

Ovation The original answer to amplifying acoustic guitars on stage, Ovation guitars were a 1970s product of US parent company Kaman's plastics expertise, using a bowl-shaped plastic back and piezo electric pick-ups to reduce amplified hum, whistle and squeal. UK distributor: Rose-Morris. Prices: high.

Shadow This German firm started life as a manufacturer of pick-ups but diversified in the '80s into guitar MIDI systems and, in the last couple of years, has introduced its own range of guitars sporting Shadow electronics, with bodies made in Italy. UK distributor: Barnes & Mullins. Prices: mid.

The Vandenberg Signature is a new top-of-the-range guitar from Peavey, who alone in recent years have managed to build American guitars to sell at oriental prices.

hardwoods for those who want all the advantages of the compact, lightweight headless style but in a more traditional 'craftsman' package. UK distributor: Soundwave. Prices: high to sky.

Steinberger Initiator of the headless bass back in the '70s, Ned Steinberger not only re-engineered the tuning systems of bass guitars, but rebuilt the whole instrument from the ground up, using active electronics and advanced structural plastics. His lightweight, compact instrument was an instant hit with bass players, and the range now includes six-strings, 12-strings, doublenecks, transposing tremolos and wood body wing designs. UK distributor: Seven Dials International. Prices: high to sky.

Sunn *See* Fender

Tokai One of *the* Japanese names in super-authentic replicas of vintage American guitars (see also Fernandes), also known for dependable low-end copies. UK distributor: Audio Equipment. Prices: low to mid.

Vox Primarily a British amplification brand, the famous Vox name has also been applied of late to a range of· Oriental guitars. UK distributor: Rose-Morris. Prices: mid.

Wal This famous name in British active basses lives on despite the premature death of founder Ian Waller in 1988. Under his direction, the Electric Wood company enjoyed a reputation for quality which attracted a whole host of top live and studio musicians to use them, and the Wal Pro continues to be one of the most desired basses around. Prices: high to sky.

Squier *See* Fender

Starforce Another Barnes & Mullins guitar line, this time of Far Eastern origin, and offering one of the best combinations of quality and cheapness the beginner could hope to find. Prices: low.

Status This important British range of active headless basses uses technology licensed from Steinberger, mated to beautifully finished bodies of selected

Washburn One of the most consistent brands to emerge from the late '70s explosion in Japanese guitars, Washburn combined American design and quality control with Japanese manufacture. Currently with a wider manufacturing base, the design initiative continues in a range that already claims to be one of the most comprehensive, with everything from acoustics through semis, electroacoustics and solid classicals to standard solids and such enterprising co-operative ventures as the Washburn Status bass. UK distributor: Washburn UK. Prices: mid to high.

Westone Another massive success story from the Far East, Westone emerged at the turn of the decade as head-on competitors for Aria with an eventually vast range of budget and mid-priced instruments which always combined value for money with fashionability. Instruments like the Thunder range broke the price barrier for active basses while top of the line guitars have consistently boasted enviable manufacturing quality. UK distributor: FCN Music. Prices: low to high.

Yamaha The world's largest musical instrument manufacturer produced, back in the '70s, probably the most serious Japanese competition for classic Gibson electrics in the form of its splendid SG range. But since the Japanese guitar boom, pricing policy seems to have worked against Yamaha electrics getting a strong UK foothold and today, despite a good and considerably rationalised range, the company's reputation for guitars is strongest in the field of acoustic instruments,

especially classical. UK distributor: Yamaha-Kemble. Prices: mid to high.

Other British brands Not massive in world market terms, many small British manufacturers are doing relatively well in the home market and therefore deserve a namecheck here. Brands to look out for include Auroc, Eccleshall, Fylde, Goodfellow, Gordon Smith, Gordy, Heartwood, Jay Dee, Kincade, Larkin, Manson, Overwater, Pangbourne and Staccato.

Other US brands Many American guitar lines prominent in the '70s or before enjoy far more limited sales outside the USA today. However, most of them are still available in Britain, if in limited quantities and with rather expensive price tags. Those with UK distributors include Dobro, G&L, Guild, Hamer, Heritage, Kramer, CF Martin, MusicMan, Paul Reed Smith, BC Rich and Schecter.

Other European brands Many guitars are made in Europe but most of those finding their way into the UK with any consistency are acoustic instruments, for example the vast classical range from the East German state-run company Demusa. However, among makers of electric instruments with UK distribution are Lag (France), Levinson (Switzerland) and Vigier (France), all with highish price tags.

Books

American Guitars – An Illustrated History, Tom Wheeler (Harper & Row)

The Complete Guitar Guide, David Lawrenson (Virgin)

The Electric Guitar – Its History And Construction, Donald Brosnac (Omnibus)

Fender Stratocaster, A R Duchossoir (Mediapresse)

Gibson Electrics, A R Duchossoir (Mediapresse)

The Gibson Guitar from 1950 – Volumes 1 & 2, Ian C Bishop (Musical New Services)

The Guitar Book, Tom Wheeler (Harper & Row)

The Guitar Handbook, Ralph Denyer (Dorling Kindersley)

Guitar Identification, A R Duchossoir (Mediapresse)

The History and Development of the American Guitar, Ken Achard (Musical New Services)

The History of Rickenbacker Guitars, Richard R Smith (Centerstream)

The Jazz Guitar – Its Evolution And Its Players, Maurice J Summerfield (Ashley Mark)

What Guitar, the Making Music staff (Track Record)

KEYBOARDS

● ▶ ● ▶ ● ▶ *You won't hear a hit record without them*

I F T H E '60s belonged to the electric guitar, the '80s belong to keyboards. From the early, 'synthy' days of the Human League, through people like OMD, Erasure, and Thomas Dolby, to bands like Frankie Goes To Hollywood (who, some would have us believe, relied almost totally on the Fairlight), keyboards of one sort or another have ruled supreme. Now, a top ten record made *without* the use of 'synths' would be unheard of; a top ten record made using them *exclusively*, commonplace.

Although the word 'synth' is bandied about as a term for describing any old piece of electronic gadgetry from a digital piano to a sampler to sequencers, it is in fact a specific term for an instrument that synthesizes (draws from many different elements to produce a whole) sound.

Unless you're planning on starting the sackbutt and crumhorn revival, the chances are you'll be dealing with 'synths' a good deal. It's not a difficult subject and even a little knowledge will save you from making the costliest mistakes like buying/hiring completely the wrong instruments, or worse, completely the wrong people.

But first some GOLDEN RULES that apply whatever type of keyboard you're dealing with.

● ● ● ● ● ● ● ▶ Only buy or use instruments that are finished and are working fully and properly. If you hear 'this feature should be implemented on version 2 software', run a mile.

● ● ● ● ● ● ● ▶ Only buy/hire instruments that contain plenty of sounds you like now. Theoretically wonderful sounds normally remain theoretical. You're left, meanwhile, with a definite waste of time and money.

● ● ● ● ● ● ● ▶ Go for instruments whose sounds are strong but universal (piano, organ), or ones that offer great flexibility. Remember, good instrumental hooks use distinctive, unusual tones. Make sure your instrument offers choice in an easy-to-achieve manner.

Pianos

Pianos are the least controversial keyboards, and they've been used on hit records since long before the electric guitar was invented. The piano has an ageless, classless sound, of which the public never seem to tire. Almost as important, it is an excellent instrument on which to write your hit; the sound having that magical blend of complexity and neutrality.

Now is not the time to analyse why, so much as what. In spite of considerable effort, manufacturers have not yet produced a totally satisfactory 'electronic' piano. On master recordings, it's always advisable to use a real acoustic piano: you'll get the best feel, the most dynamic response, and it'll help to humanise a track that might otherwise have to be filled, exclusively, with electronic instruments.

Sometimes this may not be practical, and for songwriting, routining, and certainly for playing live, you'll need to examine the following:

Despite the popularity of synths, the acoustic piano is still an excellent instrument on which to write your hit, with a sound that's a magical blend of complexity and neutrality.

Digital pianos A digital piano is simply an instrument whose piano sounds have been stored and/or created digitally – using numbers, on computer chips. In practice you don't need to worry about how the sounds are made at all, because you won't be offered programming controls. Basically, you'll either like the sound of a particular model or you won't.

Strangely enough, how a piano sounds to *you* is closely related to how it feels. If it doesn't feel like a piano, it'll be difficult to play it like a piano. If you learned piano at school you'll know that piano keys have a certain weight, and that the harder you bash them, the louder the sound. The best digital pianos recreate, using various types of artificial weighting, this feel of 'wooden-key-operating-hammer-hitting-strings'.

The sounds in most digital pianos are based around some form of sampling technology, and manufacturers delight in giving their own brand of that technology a special name: AWM, SAS, VM etc. Each one, when you read about it, will seem even more complex and unmatchable than the last so don't worry about it. Just use your ears. In addition to acoustic piano tones you can expect to find electric pianos, vibes, harpsichords, sometimes organs.

Yamaha's CVP10 clavinova is typical of today's upmarket digital pianos, styled as a home instrument but full of professional quality sounds and features, including MIDI.

Piano modules   If all you want is access to some decent piano sounds (if you're not a pianist as such, nor likely to become one), or if you already have a perfectly weighted action MIDI master keyboard, then why not try a piano module?

If the words 'piano module' mean very little to you, please read the chapter on MIDI first. Okay? Right, a piano module is simply an instrument module dedicated to piano sounds. Since about 1987, a large number have come on the market at all price ranges. Korg, Yamaha and Roland all seem to be offering excellent value models at time of writing. All use digital sounds.

Electro-acoustic pianos   Hmm. Well, in days gone by – before digital pianos came along – these were much sought after items, of which Yamaha made the most popular models, the CP70/80. Basically, 'electro-acoustic' means that the piano is an electrified acoustic, ie it has strings and hammers etc, but it also has built-in pick-ups. Being at least in part 'real' acoustic pianos, these instruments still need constant tuning (a drag) and are normally large and bulky (even bigger drag). For these reasons few continue to be made.

Fender Rhodes/Wurlitzer   Two old – and I mean *old* (b: 1968 and 1955 respectively) – and classic instruments whose sounds are sought after and much copied to this day. The original instruments themselves, however, are really as dead as mutton, though Roland's acquisition of the marque Rhodes may yet revive its career in the 1990s.

Piano samples   A sample, as the word suggests, is a snippet of something – in our context, sound. Sampling instruments are covered later on in this chapter, and to an extent they can solve your piano problems. The main drawback is that piano samples, good ones at any rate, eat vast amounts of memory so you may not have any room on your sampler to use much of anything else. If a piano sound is 'just another sound' as far as you're concerned, then a piano sample may suffice. Any larger degree of interest and it probably won't.

Buying a piano

First think about who you are and what you need. Are you a pianist? Is a piano sound the basis for all your songwriting/recording, ie are you a budding Elton John or Randy Newman? Is the look of a piano important to you? Do you want to use the instrument not only at home, for songwriting, but also for recording, and playing live? Is it just the sound of an acoustic piano you want, or do you need a whole range of piano type sounds?

List what you need and then make your way towards a dealer who can offer you some choice. Play the instrument *without* three tons of reverb and chorusing courtesy of the shop's rack of outboard gear, and check for useful things like stereo outputs, headphones socket (you may enjoy writing your hit, your neighbours may not), and any MIDI master keyboard facilities an instrument might have.

Above all, listen to the sounds. Do they inspire you, can you live with them, are they good, okay, or thin and weedy? There's little point in singling out a particular piano, since newer and mostly (though not always) better models are being launched all the time. For the aspiring hit-maker some companies are more in tune with pop/rock than others. One example is Roland, even with its HP Series, although this is primarily aimed at the domestic market. Ditto Korg with the Concert series. Current models in both series will offer a choice of sounds, pleasing action, and internal amplification. Yamaha has its Clavinova range, which is excellent though also syled towards the home market.

All three companies have produced 'rock 'n' roll type models (ie black casing and no internal amplification) in the past and will no doubt continue doing so. Of these, the Roland RD-1000 and Korg SG1 are recommended.

Buying second hand

There's not a lot to worry about here, aside from the obvious: does it look knackered? Are all the notes working? Old, old pianos – say those made before 1985 – are unlikely to sound much like an acoustic piano, and, if they have MIDI on at all, will have implemented it in rudimentary form. Provided you don't mind these limitations, go and hunt for bargains.

Costs

Pianos rarely come cheap. Constructing anything approaching a piano action keyboard is expensive; piano sounds consume memory in huge amounts.

But the investment is worthwhile. Unlike a synth, whose sounds can (easily) date – then really irritate – the sound of pianos has been around for a few hundred years and will probably continue to be so for a while longer.

Good piano modules you can pick up for as little as **£200–£300** new; for top of the range, weighted action models add another nought.

Books on pianos:

The Piano: Its Story From Zither To Grand, David Grover (Hale)

Keyfax-3 (chapter on), Julian Colbeck (Music Maker)

Organs

It shouldn't come as a shock to hear that, for the vast majority of instrument designers, programmers, and assorted hi-tech pundits, organ sounds do not occupy a great deal of their thought nowadays. If you're waiting for a *real* Hammond revival, dig in for a long night.

That said, people do still play organs; indeed the sound, though potentially dated, is still featured on the occasional hit record.

But unless you plan on being a sort of latter day Keith Emerson or Jimmy Smith, buying or hiring a dedicated organ is tantamount to madness these days. Why? Because almost every synth or sampler on the market has plenty of perfectly adequate organ sounds in them. Plus a few thousand others you'll be playing a lot more often.

If, however, you still insist on some kind of dedicated organ, then the Korg BX3 or CX3 were the best, portable, synth-type organs made. If you can find one it won't cost an arm and a leg, either. But buying a giant old Hammond is for serious enthusiasts only. And if you are, you won't need me to tell you all the pleasures and pains associated with owning one.

Synthesizers

When the first commercially viable models came on the market, synthesizers sounded, well, like synthesizers. They could only play one note at a time (and that was normally out of tune) and of their two most common tones, one was a swooshing, swizzling sound like a swarm of demented bees, and the other was a wailing trumpety sort of tone normally heard lurching between notes like it was being sick.

From these inauspicious beginnings has developed a type of instrument capable of mimicking all 'conventional' instruments and one which is used, much to the continued annoyance of the Musicians' Union, to do just that on the majority of recording sessions today.

The history of synthesizers is a long and fascinating tale – but not one you necessarily need to know now! What you do need to know now is what they are, what they can do, how much they cost, whether they're difficult to play and which ones to buy.

Think of a synthesizer as a paintbox of tone colours. Synthesizers offer you many different basic sounds, and by mixing this sound with that and stirring it up a little you can make new 'colours' of your own.

The range of sounds, and how simple the instrument makes the process of creating new ones, is obviously down to individual models, but a good synth should be able to cover the territory of bass sounds, lead line sounds, effects, brass, strings, organ . . . in other words pretty well the lot.

But that's cheating! No it's not. The most common misconception is that somehow synths can 'play' themselves without someone telling them what to do. 'Any idiot can play a synth' goes the argument. So too can any idiot play a Bosendorfer grand piano. Plink, plonk, plonk. There, it's easy.

Same goes for a synth. Rubbish in, rubbish out.

Although synthesizers can sound like a bass guitar, or a sax, what they cannot do is sound like a bass guitarist, or a saxophonist. Someone has to play the part or, if you're using a sequencer, program the part. That can be you, or you can hire someone else to do it – called a musician.

The instruments

A synthesizer is an instrument that, literally, synthesizes sound – creates a whole from a number of component parts. If you're new to the subject you may think that a synth looks like a flat sort of piano. But a keyboard is simply a triggering mechansim; synths don't have to have keyboards. A synth can just be housed in a rectangular box, and triggered by all manner of (special or specially adapted) instruments – a guitar, drum pads, things that like look like mangled saxophones, even a microphone.

The beauty of this situation – which is thanks to an electronic language called MIDI (see page 71) – is that people brought up on every instrument type, not just keyboards, can now use synths in their work.

This could prove especially important if you're on a tight budget: a guitar band, say, who need keyboard sounds can, with the necessary instruments, get those sounds themselves without having to hire a keyboard player.

Although synthesizers still come in various shapes and sizes, most nowadays, conform to the following: they're polyphonic (can play several notes at a time – like an organ, unlike a flute), they store lots of different sounds internally, and probably offer room to store more on cartridges, they're not smothered in knobs and switches (controls are 'hidden' in the software), and they're digital.

Digital vs Analogue: this debate is all but over nowadays with digital the outright winner. Although analogue models did posses a certain warmth and human quality, most digital synths have now incorporated this attribute within their own, vastly more versatile armoury.

Buying A Synth

As with pianos, any instrument in fact, recognising your own abilities and listing some of the major facilities you're after before you venture into a music store increase your chances of leaving with the instrument you need as opposed to the one you got talked into buying. So, are you:

1   An experienced keyboard player looking for another synth?

2   A piano player looking for a first synth?

3   New to keyboard playing but proficient on another instrument?

4   New to playing an instrument altogether?

And would you describe yourself as:

A   A boffin?

B   Quite technical (car servicing, avid computer user etc)?

C   Can wire up a plug but not particularly technical?

D   'Technically' brain-dead?

Okay, if you've honed in on **4D**, a tactful suggestion might be that you look at another instrument (drums, perhaps); all others will find a wide choice today.

If you're in group . . .

1 Just keep abreast of what's available but don't take instrument fads too seriously (if everyone's got one, then everyone's going to be using the same sounds – boring).

2 Spend a lot of time listening to the different sounds a synth is capable of. Make sure you like what you hear now (never mind when you've spent four years programming the thing), and make sure those sounds are the types of sounds you'll really use. Don't be overly impressed by 'effect' sounds. Good, strong, but interesting musical tones will be far more useful.

3 Depending on whether you're looking to become a keyboard player or simply trigger a synth from your own instrument type, save money and space by looking at synth modules *only*. If you're not a keyboard player (and don't want to become one) why bother buying a synth with a keyboard? If you do fancy learning a little, however, don't fall into the trap of buying synths with mini or reduced-size keys. They may seem attractive initially but they'll murder any technique you may acquire in the long run. It may also be worth considering a home synth – one that offers some help in terms of built-in drum machine, sequencer etc. Such instruments are not the toys they were a few years ago.

4 Difficult. It all depends upon how seriously you want to be able to play any instrument. Avoid small-key models unless you're under the age of six, and

look for instruments that encourage you (as opposed either to making you work really hard to find some good sounds, or to instruments that do all the work for you – you may as well listen to your stereo).

If you describe yourself as ...

A You probably don't need our help at all.

B All current synths are well within your grasp, not only in operational terms but in new-sound programming.

C You'll be fine. Synths require patience more than brain cells.

D It may be rather hard going but remember, few popsters are *Mastermind* candidates and, if you're even vaguely successful, you can always hire in a programmer to do your dirty work for you. All the same, make sure you can at least switch on, change sounds, and sort out a few basic MIDI functions before you part with cash. Avoid American synths as these tend to be more complex and long-winded than Japanese.

Yamaha's DX7 II-D is one of the latest versions of a classic instrument – the DX7 FM digital synthesiser which revolutionised the sound of pop and rock music in the early '80s.

No one synth or one manufacturer is going to help you have a hit record more than any other. But a synth you understand, and can work with, will both help you be more creative and 'inspire' you to keep working.

Sound is inspiring. Listen to all your potential purchase's presets, and ask what facilities there are for more sounds (on cartridge/disk). How easy is it to 'tweak' sounds, if not actually program new ones?

Finally, although you should look at specifications and listen to what the experts say, *Trust your ears*.

Costs

A professional synth that you won't tire of in two weeks is still not an expensive item, say upwards of **£600**. At the top end you shouldn't need to pay more than **£1,500**. A synth stuffed with too much extraneous gadgetry is best avoided.

Buying second hand

This is a far less hazardous excercise than it used to be; few synths now contain such troublesome things as voltage controlled oscillators. Courtesy of the computer chip, modern instruments are a lot more stable.

As a matter of course you should still: Test all outputs and make sure they a deliver clean signal.

Test all moving parts (knobs/sliders) to make sure they don't crackle and pop on being used (though switch cleaner should clear up the trouble if they do).

You should also: Check, on synths made before 1985, that the MIDI implementation is sufficient for your needs. MIDI only came into being in late 1983 and it took two or three years for things to settle down.

Check (if the instrument has the facility) that sound cartridges are still available.

Books on synths (and programming)

The Complete DX7(II), Howard Massey (Amsco)

The New Complete Synthesizer, David Crombie (Omnibus)

Synthesizers For Musicians, RA Penfold (PC Publishing)

A Synthesist's Guide To Acoustic Instruments, Howard Massey (Amsco)

FM Theory & Applications, John Chowning & Dave Bristow (Yamaha)

Synthesizers and Computers, staff of Keyboard magazine (Hal Leonard)

The Secrets of Analog & Digital Synthesis, Steve de Furia & Joe Scacciaferro (Hal Leonard)

Synthesizer Techniques, staff of Keyboard magazine (Hal Leonard)

Keyfax-3, Julian Colbeck (Music Maker Books)

Videos

DX7 Programming/Advanced DX7 Programming, Ronnie Lawson (Hot Licks)

Multi-Keyboard Master Class, David Rosenthal (Hot Licks)

The Secrets of Analog & Digital Synthesis, Steve de Furia & Joe Scacciaferro (Ferro Technologies)

Chick Corea Keyboard Workshop, (DCI Video)

George Duke, Keyboard Improvisation, (DCI Video)

Samplers

Sampling – the business of digitally recording a sound in order to re-trigger (play) it, musically, from a keyboard, drum pads, or a sequencer – was first seen in the early 1980s as one of many functions on the Fairlight, a house-priced workstation 'instrument' from Australia.

American company E-Mu spotted its potential and swiftly produced a dedicated sampling instrument called the Emulator, after which the whole process began to take off in a big way.

Sampling's original application, that of 'recording' notes from, say, a sax or a guitar in order to play the sound of that sax or guitar from a keyboard (or suitably equipped MIDI controller), was soon joined by the novelty angle, 'playing' barking dogs and breaking glass etc.

All well and good. But as time went on and sampling instruments became both cheaper and more powerful, so their application shifted from that of simply snatching the sound of certain instruments/effects, to snatching whole sections of songs – normally other people's (hit) songs!

The problem is that sampling a 'hook' from an old hit and incorporating it into your own song is dead easy to do, it gives your own song an instant degree of familiarity (as if it's a hit already) and it's undeniably catchy. Whether it will prove to be illegal as opposed to just immoral is still for the courts to decide.

In its worst form (swiping entire chunks of someone else's material), most would agree that sampling is a supremely rotten and uncreative pastime. In other cases, like swiping a particularly catchy sounding snare drum (Tony Thompson's on Bowie's 'Let's Dance', for instance, which has been plundered without mercy), you come up against the argument that 'a sound' is in the public domain. You can't copyright a sound – at least you can't *yet*.

'Rapid gunfire' sampling (an effect created by repeatedly triggering a note, as a trill, then holding the note down so that the entire sample and not just the front end of it plays), first graced a hit record on Paul Hardcastle's 'N-n-n-n-nineteen' but has truly came of age on late '80s dance music like House and Hip Hop.

The instruments

User sampling, especially on something like a grand piano – in order to have it playable across an entire keyboard span – can be a complex and fiddly business. Provided you don't mind using previously-sampled sounds, though (from sample 'libraries' you've bought or nicked), using a sampler is dead easy. All you have to do is load in your desired sounds off disk.

Almost all models use one of two disk sizes: 3.5 inch and 2.8 inch Quick Disk. Unless you are really strapped for cash, always go for instruments using the 3.5 inch disks as they can hold far more data and are much less hassle. Although most companies produce instruments using 3.5 inch disks, the disks themselves are not compatible.

The quality, availability, and range of an instrument's sample library becomes of great importance. Akai samplers, in particular the S-900/950/1000 instruments, are exceptionally well-endowed with sound disks. Always check into the state of an instrument's sound library before you buy.

Aside from the obvious, there's no difference between a keyboard sampler and a sample module. That said, many manufacturers release the 'module of the instrument' after the full keyboard version, by which time they've made some improvements. You'll often find that the modular version is priced identically, but trades the keyboard and casing for an increased memory. This is a good deal.

If you're going to get serious about sampling – like play around with whole sections of songs, turn them upside down etc – then a workstation type of instrument such as Commander's Lynex or Hybrid Arts' ADAP might best fit the bill.

Sampling off CD

For legal, never mind moral, reasons, it's impossible to recommend that you sample other people's material off CD in order to incorporate it into your own music. Unless – and this does happen – you square things with the artist/publisher in question. If you just want to sample a particularly good drum sound or bass sound, the reality is that no-one, even if they wanted to, can catch you or prevent you from doing so.

But there's a danger that if too many sounds are re-cycles of re-cycles of re-cycles, music will eventually stagnate. Indeed some say it has already.

Original sounds help sell records. Sampling, used creatively, is a perfect medium for producing new and exciting sounds. Use it.

Sample replay instruments

Conversely, if you're not going to do much/any sampling yourself, then don't bother buying facilities you won't use and opt for a sample replay instrument such as, currently, E-Mu's Proteus or Roland's U-110, which contain hundreds of different instrument samples but offer no user sampling at all.

Buying a sampler – Look out for:

●●●●●●●➤ Multi-timbral capability (see page 73)
●●●●●●●➤ Separate voice outputs
●●●●●●●➤ SCSI (to hook up with hard disk for mass storage)
●●●●●●●➤ Good sample rate (40kHz and above)
●●●●●●●➤ Large internal memory (1 kbyte and above)

Costs

You can spend as little as **£100** on a sampler, or as much as **£100,000**. The difference between them concerns two things primarily: sound quality and power.

On a **£100** sampler you'll be able to record yourself going 'Do!' or 'Ah' and you can play it back okay (d-d-d-d-d-do! etc) even if it does sound a bit like you're talking under water. And that's about your lot.

On a **£100,000** instrument you could probably sample several minutes of sparkling, CD quality stereo sound, plus have an entire library of sounds on tap, and be able to cut and paste within, reverse, turn upside down, transpose, and process the entire assembled track any way you want.

In between you have a whole army of instruments, priced a little higher than the average synth (**£1,200–£2,000**). Unless you've either had several hits or you're flat broke, these are the instruments you're looking for.

Books on sampling (instruments)

The Sampling Book, Steve de Furia & Joe Scacciaferro (Hal Leonard)
Casio FZ-1 & FZ-10M, Steve de Furia & Joe Scacciaferro (Hal Leonard)

Sampler Setups: Ensoniq Mirage, Terry Fryer (Hal Leonard)
Sampler Setups: Casio FZ-1, Terry Fryer (Hal Leonard)

Sequencers

If you think you can make a hit record without using some sort of sequencer, then you must be a) of the Frank Sinatra generation, b) an obsessively traditional folk group, or c) naive.

The thing is that sequencers, once the sterile bane of 'real' musicians' lives, have come on such a lot from the days of 'Don't You Want Me?' or 'Won't Get Fooled Again' that they are standard fare on almost all recordings. Using a sequencer does not mean you have to sound like Kraftwerk; it does not mean that everything will get churned out in strict, metronomic monotony; sequencers just co-ordinate and simplify recording, and in doing so will save you large amounts of time and money.

What is a sequencer?

A sequencer is a recording device that instead of recording music, records data ('play this note, now, with this amount of vibrato . . .') which is then turned into music by instruments connected to it.

Like a multitrack tape recorder, a modern sequencer will offer a number of different tracks. On track 1, say, data concerning a bass line can be stored; on track 2 data concerning a piano part, and so on. . . . On playback, all the parts will be in sync (synchronised).

Sequencers deal in data as opposed to music. They can only work with instruments that can be triggered electronically *without the aid of a human being* – in other words things like synths and drum machines, but not electric guitars.

You cannot sing into a sequencer, and neither (amazingly enough!) will it trigger your voice. Nor any acoustic instrument.

Nowadays all sequencers are based around a language called MIDI (see page 71) and, with few exceptions, if an instrument has MIDI, it can be used with sequencers and if it hasn't, it cannot.

If this all sounds rather limiting, just consider that there are MIDI wind instruments, MIDI guitars, MIDI drum pads (as well as drum machines), there's even a MIDI player piano (Yamaha), and of course MIDI samplers which can faithfully capture any sound you like – including vocals. Anything missing? No.

Sequencer types

1   A synth/sampler with a built-in sequencer.

2   A dedicated sequencer.

3   Sequencing software on a personal computer.

Type 1   Though in some ways the easiest to figure out since you have no connections to make, a built-in sequencer is normally limited in terms of note capacity and editing facilities. Most are best kept to use as an 'ideas' scratchpad.

Type 2   A sequencer and nothing but a sequencer, this type is now facing severe competition from option number 3. Advantages include comparative ease of use and portability; disadvantages include price (you're spending quite a lot of money on a device that can only do one thing – be a sequencer), lack of updatability (with a few notable exceptions such as Roland's MRC-500) and small display screens.

Type 3   The modern approach, but one with plenty of hidden costs, such as the host computer, monitor and (using most computers) a MIDI-computer interface. However, the advantages of being able to see a whole screen's worth of information at a time, a large number of record tracks, extensive editing, and often direct links into musical notation, management and instrument editing programs, more than justify the added expense.

Roland's MC500 Microcomposer is a sophisticated compositional tool which, unlike most dedicated sequencers, is software-updatable – meaning it's always state-of-the-art.

Right: The modern approach to sequencing is to buy a software package for your computer. Steinberg's Cubit (now renamed Cubase for copyright reasons) is one of the most powerful available.

Leading computers for which sequencing software is written

Amiga: is becoming popular thanks to its multitasking (being able to run several programs at once) capability.

Apple Macintosh: is the best if you can afford it.

Atari 520ST/1040ST: has the largest selection of software, good price, good graphics.

BBC: is an older computer with only one serious-application package still in use, called UMI.

Commodore 64: was once the greatest, but now no pro would give it a second glance. Plenty of cheap sequencing programs still around though.

IBM (or IBM compat): has some good programs available but hasn't shaken off its rather 'businessy' image. Note: Yamaha C1 computer is IBM compatible.

Leading sequencing programs include: Pro 24 from Steinberg, Creator/Notator from C-Lab, SMPTE-track from Hybrid Arts, Performer from Mark Of The Unicorn, Master Tracks Pro from Passport and KCS from Dr T's.

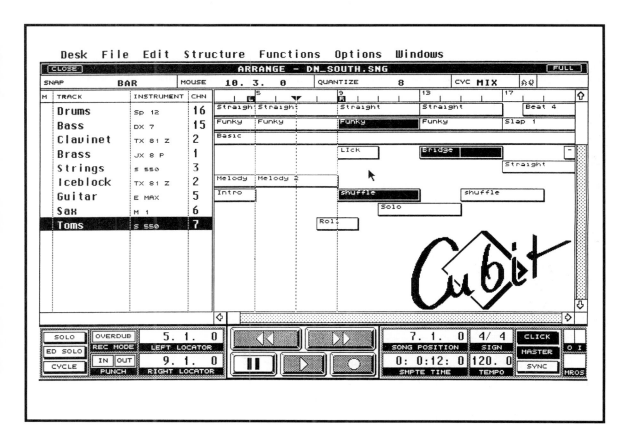

Why sequencers?

1   Do you play bass, guitar, keyboards, drums, sax, violin? If you can, can you play them all at the same time? If no to the first question, can you call on all such instrumentalists, free, at all hours of the day and night? Right. So, provided you have access to suitable sounds (a sampler, a synth) and you yourself are reasonably musical, a sequencer will allow you to use all instrument types in your work. In other words as a single person you can produce a complete band/orchestral arrangement.

2   A sequencer not only gives you complete flexibility when it comes to writing the bare bones of a song (you can transpose it, slow it down, change parts around etc in seconds), but it continues to offer the same flexibility when it comes to the final arrangement.

3   Working with a sequencer at home, you can write and arrange a song for, well, no cost at all except your own electricity. Instead of working from scratch in the studio you can then take an almost complete song, on which, say, you need only to add vocals, then mix. Not only does this remove studio clock-watching panic, but it will save you a fortune.

4   Working with a sequencer does not mean everything will sound sterile and lifeless. Modern sequencers are capable of great subtlety, and can be injected with uncanny degrees of 'humanity'. However, they don't drink, don't turn up late, and they don't make mistakes.

Books

Setups: Roland MC-500, Terry Fryer (Hal Leonard)

The Complete Guide to MIDI Software, Howard Massey (Amsco)

Home keyboards

'Home', 'single', 'portable' keyboards – call them what you will – would not appear, on the face of it, to have any place in a book about how to make a hit record.

You probably think of this breed of instrument (invented by Casio and growing out of the home organ business) only in terms of Christmas, and of High Street electrical retailers being stuffed to the gills with them.

But there are home keyboards and home keyboards. Up at the top end you'll find instruments whose musical sounds rival any 'serious' synth and whose drum sounds equal most drum machines. These instruments simply go on to offer a degree of help in the shape of pre-programmed accompaniment patterns, built-in speakers etc.

Such instruments, the current crop of which include the AX7 from Technics, E-10/20 from Roland, and Yamaha's PSR6300, are ideal for non keyboard players (even non instrumentalists) who need some form of technical help but are nonetheless not unmusical, nor below the age of 10, nor deaf!

In particular, Roland's E-10/20 boasts an array of accompaniment patterns that have 'hit' written all over them. Quite superb.

Several recent home keyboards have sounds to rival 'serious' synths and drum machines. One such, Roland's E-20, offers a seductive array of 'instant hit' accompaniments.

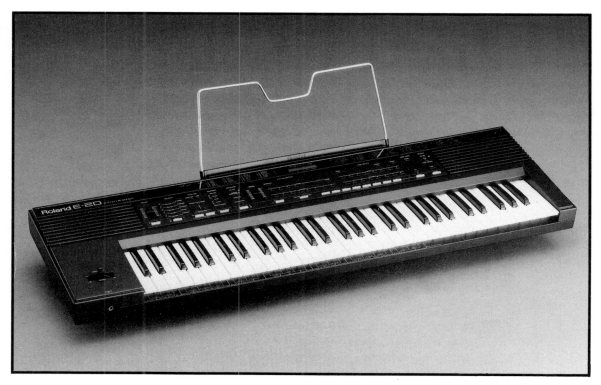

Who's Who –
a guide to the
major keyboard
manufacturers

Akai Founded in 1929 as a manufacturer of electric motors (later moving on to tape machines and hi-fi), this mid-size Japanese company started producing musical instruments in 1984. Now making a whole range of keyboard gear, Akai's biggest success to date has been with samplers; the S-900 and the more recent S-1000, both of which were co-designed in England and the US, setting the pace for the whole of the genre. Akai also works with American drum machine guru Roger Linn, producing top of the range sampling drum machines and sequencers, and in 1988 launched the world's most cost-effective digital multi-track recorder, ADAM. Typically, Akai instruments are stylish; mid to high price.

Casio Having already swamped the world with watches and calculators, Casio took the instrument world by storm in 1980 by introducing the concept of the low cost 'home' keyboard, which went on to sell by the bucketload. Although Casio scored a hit in the mid 1980s with the CZ range of digital synths, the company didn't start making fully professional instruments until 1987, which saw the release of the FZ-1 sampler. Athough the bulk of Casio's keyboard business continues to come from low cost instruments – home synths, plus the occasional piano – the company's high end products should in no way be dismissed as inferior or cheaply made.

E-Mu Although E-Mu was not the first to offer sampling on an instrument (that was Fairlight), this young Californian company did produce the first dedicated sampler in 1980 called the Emulator. Subsequent success came with the E-II and to a lesser extent the E-III – expensive, hi-tech beasts both – and with a line of sample-based drum machines. In 1989, E-Mu launched its first mid-to-low price instrument, Proteus, a sample replay module. To date, the company has stuck to sampling technology like a limpet; indeed it has yet to produce an instrument based on anything else. Though E-Mu's design skill and originality have never been in question, some products have proved temperamental in the past. Things do seem to be improving however.

Ensoniq This punchy American company shot to fame in 1985 with the Mirage, the first keyboard sampler to hit the streets at a price you could afford. Some say Ensoniq (founded in 1982 by some ex-execs from Commodore) has never scrambled to such giddy heights since, but in fact the company's diversification into synths, and more recently into the world of homey digital pianos, has been quite a success. Interestingly, while most other companies are reducing their quantities of high end instruments, Ensoniq, who began life producing the bargain-priced Mirage, has steadily moved up-market. Early products were made in Italy; now everything is US assembled even though some parts (such as the keyboards) remain Italian.

Kawai Established as long ago as 1929, Kawai is a very large, traditional Japanese company that spends most of its time and energy building acoustic pianos and electric organs, and running music schools. When the company finally discovered hi-tech in the late 1980s, however, it did so with considerable flair and success. Kawai may still lack the innovative powers of a Roland or a Yamaha but it produces professional and reliable equipment, generally at tempting prices. Notable successes include the R-50 drum machine, and K1(II) synth.

Korg As the name suggests, Korg began life as an organ manufacturer, doing so in the 1960s. Establishing itself in the fields of synths and drum machines by the early 1970s, the company entrenched itself in the middle ground, producing instruments that were neither house-price expensive nor toy-class cheap. Notable successes of the period include the Poly-800 synth and BX/CX-3 organs. In 1986 Yamaha acquired a 40 per cent stake in Korg, after which the company has gone from strength to strength – not only in such familiar territories as synths, with the world-beating M1(R), but also in new areas such as a digital pianos with the P3 piano module and the continually expanding Concert series. A company on the up.

Kurzweil With all its products still based around the high-priced 250 sampler, Kurzweil's re-packaging prowess has enabled it to survive since it was started in the early 1980s. So far this American company – currently employing the legendary Bob Moog – has made synths, pianos, master keyboards, and recently a series of modules (containing '250' sounds), all of which, though good, are invariably costly by the time they reach the UK.

Oberheim One of the leading lights of synth development during the '70s, Oberheim is but a shadow of its former self today: even Tom Oberheim has left! While all around moved into digital synthesis, Oberheim has remained doggedly loyal to analogue, a move that in part explains its current status. Though some older Oberheim synths contain much sought-after sounds, the instruments themselves are rarely reliable enough to warrant much outlay of cash. Newer products, with few exceptions, tend to be of esoteric value too.

Roland Easily the most successful dedicated rock/pop instrument company (Yamaha's scope is far wider), Roland is still a tiny and very personal company in its homeland of Japan. Founded in 1972, Roland has always come across as a real *musician's* company, producing a wide range of reliable products – keyboards, amps, drum machines, guitar synths – at affordable prices. (Pedals and amps are also made under the name of Boss.) High spots include the unbeatable Juno-60 analogue synth, Hip-Hop's favourite drum machine the TR-808, the MC-500 sequencer, and currently LA synthesis synths in the shape of the D50, D10/20, D5 etc. Roland's reputation for product knowledge and helping the public to sort out 'gear' problems is unmatched.

Technics As part of the giant Matsushita corporation, Technics has the potential to be the world's largest producer of musical instruments. Aside from occasional forays into the world of hi-tech with such instruments as the PX1/7/5 digital pianos, the company has concentrated on the organ and home keyboard market. Signs of change came in 1988 with the AX series home synths. Good value instruments if, to date, lacking in the hipness dept!

Yamaha Celebrating its centenary in 1987, Yamaha produces an almost complete range of musical equipment. In the early days of synthesis, Yamaha synths had a reputation for being good but slightly dull and rather overpriced, a label that changed overnight in 1983 thanks to the DX7 – the world's best-selling synth *ever*. Although Yamaha has had great mileage out of DX7-type instruments (the technology spilling over into home keyboards and pianos), a new direction is bound to emerge by the 1990s. Though not all Yamaha keyboards become world-beaters (a weird company trait is to launch instruments in pairs – one great, one not so great, so as to make the first one look even greater!) you are as assured of value and reliability as much it is ever possible to be.

DRUM MACHINES

•▶•▶••▶ *An almost immovable part of musical life*

DRUM machines have had an enormous effect on hitmaking. Before their existence there was no way people could make demos *at home* (how can I set up/record/play real drums?) never mind master whole tracks in the studio without the help of anyone else.

With their unwavering time-keeping, impossible-to-play patterns, and, recently, access to hitherto unimaginable noises-as-drum-sounds thanks to the power of sampling, drum machines have also influenced music itself.

Acoustic drums are still a vital element of live music, as exemplified by U2's Larry Mullen with his Yamaha Turbo Custom kit. But few drummers ever have hits in their own right.

Listen to the hits of the '60s and '70s and you'll hear erratic time keeping, tom fills that get lost, other sounds that *should* have got lost. But the records seem to have a certain character which is missing on so many hits of the '80s whose drum sounds, bloated and extravagant though they may be, are nonetheless identical to everyone else's, and which sport patterns you could set your watch by.

Although it's unlikely we'll return to the more human days of pre drum machine, the question of samey sounds can, and many feel will, be looked at more closely in the future. We know that the brain eventually learns to ignore or phase out constant or repetitive sounds like a ticking clock or a humming fridge. The danger is that drum machines, with their invariably identically struck sounds, will eventually bore the public into the ground; the things that stimulate the brain being change, variation – even the most subtle shifts in timing and velocity will do.

So be warned: drum machines have become an almost immovable part of musical life – from writing and demoing to mastering and performing – but unless people start using them creatively, which is quite possible, then the damage they could do in terms of general boredom with pop/rock music may prove a far more lasting effect.

What is a drum machine?

A drum machine is a box full of drum and percussion sounds with a computer inside that can assemble said sounds into patterns and, eventually, complete drum tracks. Patterns are normally built up by tapping individual instrument 'pads' to a metronome accompaniment. Using a series of computer-like commands given to you from a display screen patterns can then be joined together to form a song. Almost all current drum machines use digital sounds, and some offer on-board sampling too.

The instruments

Most drum machines conform to a style: they have pads to which you can assign various instruments, they have smallish display screens to help with programming, and they are generally not difficult to operate.

At the low end of the market you can still expect to find good quality, realistic sounding drums, but with limitations as to the number and range of sounds, and limited memory in which to store completed drum tracks. For writing/demoing purposes, such things really shouldn't matter.

But, if you want to take your home-programmed drum tracks any further – mastering or live playing – then you should look towards instruments that offer more sophisticated editing facilities, separate outputs for individual drum

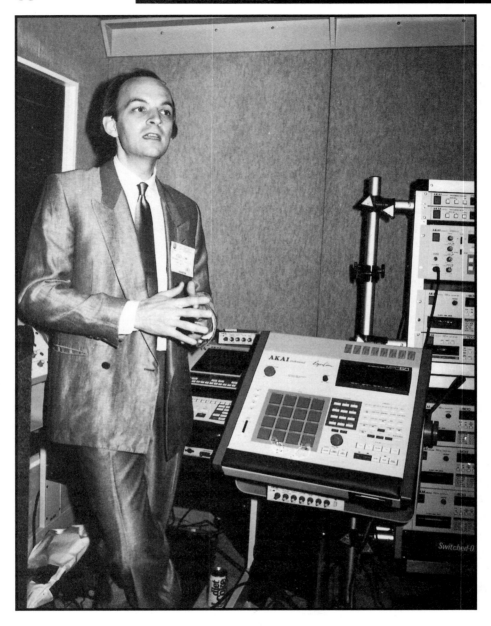

Roger Lin, father of the modern digital drum machine, with his current Akai-sponsored creation, the ASQ60.

sounds, and perhaps even a choice of synchronisation standards (FSK, Sync, MIDI, MTC, SMPTE).

At the very top come drum machines which not only offer a wide and high class range of built-in drum sounds but also offer user sampling, so your own 'custom' sounds can get in on the act. In one sense this is the ideal. But it has to be said that a dedicated sampler triggered by a sequencer may be able to offer these facilities in an ultimately more flexible manner.

Traditionally, American drum machines from such companies as Alesis, Linn (no longer in existence but still producing as Akai/Linn) and E-Mu have far more powerful and dynamic-sounding drum sounds than their Japanese counterparts.

Electronic drums

Electronic drum is not another name for drum machine. They are two totally separate things. You hit electronic drums with sticks; the drums themselves can be pads, or you can use contact mikes on acoustic drums which go on to trigger drum sounds from the 'brain'. You'll play electronic drums as well as you play acoustic drums. With a drum machine, you need no manual drumming skills, just a feel for what constitutes a good drum pattern – something that is still no mean feat.

Buying a drum machine

Bearing in mind this chapter's opening remarks, it may be wise to look out for drum machines that offer flexibility. In terms of sound this can either be a facility for updating sounds using cards or new chips, a facility for fine-tuning internal sounds (in tone and decay, as well as pitch), or even a degree of user sampling.

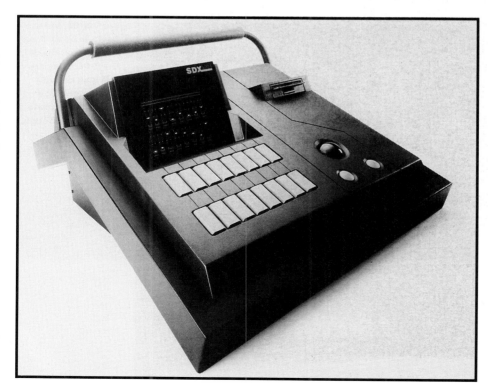

Simmons' SDX promised to be the ultimate percussion computer system, but it arrived too late in a changing market to save this famous British company from liquidating in May '89.

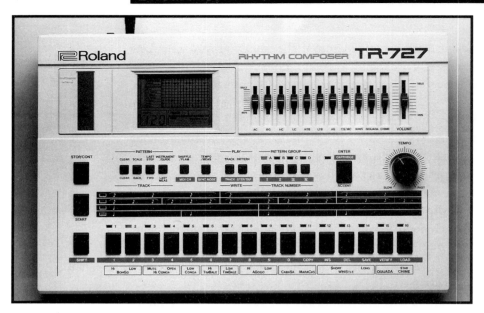

Drum machines like the Roland TR-727 have had an enormous effect on hitmaking, but, now more than ever, they must be used more creatively to avoid boredom-inducing predictability.

Acoustic drums may have received a knocking from drum machines and electronic drums in the 1980s, but they seem to be making a good comeback in the '90s. They are still instruments that accompany rather than create hit records, though.

Separate instrument outputs are a must for all proper studio applications, and SMPTE reading-writing may be invaluable. (SMPTE is a professional time-based code used for synchronisation purposes in almost all recording studios.)

Other useful features to look out for include a 'repeat' function for simple programming of rolls, and 'offset', which can be used to change timings within a track and so, perhaps, minimise the monotony hazard.

Buying second hand

Some older drum machines, such as Roland's TR-606 and 808, have become collector's items thanks to their renewed hipness value at the hands of Acid House and Hip Hop, styles that have taken these pre-*digital* drum machine sounds – lightweight and synthetic though they are – to heart.

The problem with second hand drum machines is not so much their sounds as their compatibility with more recent equipment. We now take for granted such features as MIDI Song Pointers (which, when using a drum machine with a sequencer, ensure the two follow each other, bar by bar, as opposed to merely keeping in time), but plenty of MIDI drum machines were made without this feature.

Costs

Entry level digital drum machines range from **£200–300** upwards. A good professional specification instrument should cost only around **£500–600**, but models filled with user sampling and SMPTE functions invariably break the four figure mark – by quite a long way.

Books on drum machines

Set-ups: Roland TR-505, Terry Fryer (Hal Leonard)
260 Drum Machine patterns, Rene-Pierre Bardet (Hal Leonard)
Roland Drum Machine Rhythm Dictionary, Sandy Feldstein (Alfred Pubs)
Electronic Drums, Steve Tarshis & Frank Vilardi (Amsco)
The Complete Electronic Percussion Book, David Crombie (Amsco)
The Complete Simmons Drum Book, Bob Henrit (Wise Pubs)

Drum machine manufacturers

Almost without exception, drum machines are made by the same hi-tech companies that make keyboards – see Chapter 4, page 62.

Acoustic drums

While drums, rhythm and percussion are all essential ingredients of a hit record, the fact that drum machines can be used by non-drummers and have been considerably influential both in style and approach to record making has resulted in their detailed inclusion at the expense of regular acoustic drums.

There are many star drummers, of course, and few star drum machine operators. But none of the former has made his name as hitmaker through being a drummer. Phil Collins came to worldwide domination as a performer/songwriter, Mick Fleetwood as a band leader, Ringo as a Beatle etc.

It must be recognised, therefore, that playing acoustic drums – no matter how brilliantly – is likely to gain you a reputation in the business, lots of work, features in the drum magazines . . . but few hit records, unless you sing, write songs or happen to play in a band with other members who can.

MIDI

●◆●◆●◆ *A universal 'chat line' for musical equipment*

PRESSED to say whether you really need to know about MIDI, the answer would have to be no. In the same way as you don't need to know how a tape recorder works, or a mixing desk.

But MIDI has opened doors, and made hits possible, for all sorts of people who wouldn't otherwise have had the money or expertise to write, develop, and complete production of their own music.

From all the talk, magazine articles, books, and even videos on the subject, it's clear that MIDI is in danger of becoming an end in itself; especially for the boffin brigade.

Fine if that's what turns you on. But MIDI's practical applications are perfectly comprehensible to anyone (even complete technovices) prepared to sit down for just a few minutes and have them explained. It is not that difficult.

MIDI stands for Musical Instrument Digital Interface, an awful lot of wordage for what was originally designed as a simple, universal language allowing previously unconnectable instruments to be connected – on the face of it, the necessity of which you'd be perfectly forgiven for questioning.

But thanks to MIDI, the power of dedicated computers is now fully incorporated into the musical scene. Guitarists can 'play' synth sounds, drummers can 'play' guitar samples, people like Jean-Michel Jarre can gesticulate wildly on stage and thus 'play' *anything*, lighting rigs can be controlled by sequencers . . . just about anything can operate anything else.

The point being, that no matter who made a particular piece of gear – Roland or Yamaha or Simmons etc – if it's got MIDI on it, it's joined the club, so to speak.

Like any club there are rules and regulations, MIDI's being written out in a document called the *MIDI Spec 1.0*. These simply say that if you want to perform a certain task, 'please do it like this'. It cannot be any more dictatorial because each manufacturer must remain free to design its instruments the way it wants.

MIDI's most physical manifestation is a five pin din socket, normally in multiples of three seen on the back of 'MIDI' instruments under the headings In, Out, and Thru.

If you connect 'MIDI' instruments together, via these sockets and special MIDI leads, then some form of communication will be possible. Precisely what sort of communication that will be depends upon the instruments in question and how their various pieces of MIDI data have been set up.

For example, you have two synths. You stick a lead in the MIDI Out socket of one and shove it in the MIDI In socket of the other. Without doing anything else other than switching them both on and making sure both have audio leads trailing out towards an amp, when you play the synth with the MIDI Out socket connected, *both* synths will 'sound'.

Replace the first synth with a MIDI guitar and the guitar will 'play' the synth. Ditto drum pads, MIDI mikes, anything, in fact, that has a MIDI Out and some form of triggering mechanism – something you can hit, pluck, or blow.

So what's
going on?

What's going on is simply that millions of little digital messages (combinations of 'ons' and 'offs' expressed in binary computer language as ones and zeros) are zooming out of the *controlling* MIDI instrument, down the lead, into the *slave* MIDI instrument and telling it what to do, as in 'okay we have a note being played here, it's a Middle C, and now it's stopped' and stuff like that.

That's clever enough, but the really clever part comes in how MIDI organises itself so that several instruments can be connected, and so that you can control certain parts of an instrument and not others.

Although there are many different aspects of MIDI, knowledge of just two will get you a long way. The first concerns MIDI Modes.

A MIDI Mode is a state of being: in one Mode you can accomplish a certain set of tasks, in another, another set.

MIDI started off using four basic Modes, with a fifth – wouldn't you know it currently the most important – sort of sneaking in the back door sometime around 1987. This fifth Mode is the one to understand and it's called Multi Mode, which you'll find implemented on instruments that are 'multi-timbral.'

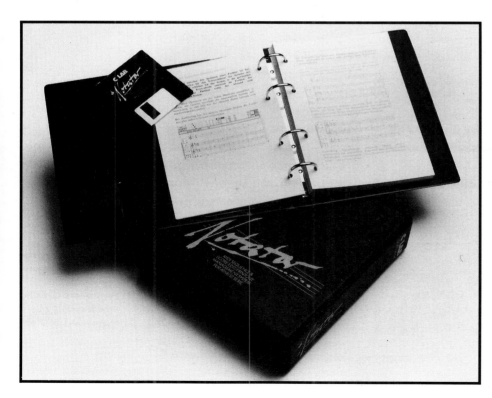

Personal computers are now fully part of the hit-making team. Notator, from German company C-Lab, is proving the most popular Atari ST-based sequencer program at present.

This means that the instrument is capable of sounding several different voices simultaneously, for instance a synth on which you can play, say, drum sounds, bass sounds, brass etc all at the same time.

A multi-timbral synth is very useful because it'll save you money, space and time since you won't have to buy, store, and learn how to use so many different instruments.

Closely related to multi-timbralism is the business of MIDI channels. Eh? Like your TV, MIDI can 'pick up' signals on different channels. Switch channels and you'll get a different picture/instrument coming through. MIDI offers 16 channels.

In Multi Mode each individual sound can be controlled on its own MIDI channel, whether you're triggering it from a sequencer or from some form of human-based controller like a keyboard, MIDI drum pads or MIDI wind instrument.

If you are simply connecting three non-multi-timbral synths, then if you set each to their own MIDI channel, switching channels on your controller will harness each, separately, in turn.

In terms of how you do these things, every MIDI instrument will have a specific set of MIDI controls, using which you can switch channels and change modes.

The level of MIDI control (what you can do using MIDI) varies considerably from instrument to instrument. Some offer plain 'yes you can hook me up but that's it' control while others' MIDI features would fill 50 pages.

This is about all you need to know to get by. The more you know, the more you can accomplish (though be warned, the more you can also waste time).

MIDI controllers
include:

Keyboards Any MIDI keyboard can be used as a controller but there are also dedicated controllers, ie *all* they do is control. The best known are the Yamaha KX88 (old, but nice action), Roland A50/80 (advanced and new), and

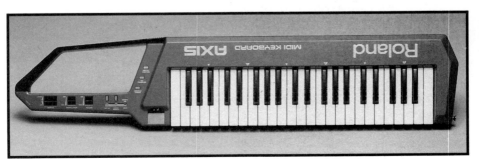

Roland's Axis is one of several sling-on keyboard controllers offering new freedom of movement on stage.

Cheetah MK5V (budget priced). There are also 'sling-on' guitar type keyboard controllers, among which are the Yamaha KX-5 (simple, low cost) and Roland Axis (advanced).

Drums   Many companies now produce MIDI drum pads including such 'keyboard' companies as Roland, Casio, and Yamaha, plus dedicated drum manufacturers like Simmons (recently, and sadly, defunct) and D-Drum. Also made are contact mikes that you can attach to regular acoustic drums, the signal from which is turned into MIDI data by an accompanying 'black box'. All current drum machines are MIDI-based.

Courtney Pine was one of the first sax players to recognise the potential offered by Yamaha's WX7 wind controller when linked via MIDI to a variety of FM digital sound sources.

Wind MIDI wind instruments are relatively new, the pace being set by Yamaha with the WX7, and Akai with the sax-like EWI and trumpet-like EVI instruments. Casio produce a couple of digital horns which, though looking like toys and also having built-in sounds, can operate as controllers.

Guitar Pure MIDI guitars are quite few and far between. Most common are either guitar synths which happen to be based on MIDI, or MIDI kits that you can attach to your own instrument. Top guitar synths are made by Roland, Yamaha, and recently Casio; kits by Roland, Korg and Shadow.

Books on MIDI include:

Practical MIDI Handbook, RA Penfold (PC Publishing)

What's MIDI, [various] (Track Record)

The MIDI Book, Steve de Furia & Joe Scacciaferro (Hal Leonard)

The MIDI Resource Book, Steve de Furia & Joe Scacciaferro (Hal Leonard)

The MIDI Implementation Book, Steve de Furia & Joe Scacciaferro (Hal Leonard)

MIDI The Ins Outs and Thrus, Jeff Rona (Hal Leonard)

MIDI For Musicians, Craig Anderton (AMSCO)

RECORDING –
THE CRAFT

●▶●▶●▶ *A means to an end or an end to your means?*

YOU CAN have a hit record without writing the song. You can have a hit record without owning or indeed playing an instrument. Hits have been had without the aid of managers, publicists, the press, the lot. But you can't, fairly obviously, have a hit record without going into some sort of studio, somehow, somewhere, and recording it.

There are degrees of course. Pop stars of old could 'cut a record' in a morning. A singer would hear the song live, on the piano, get handed the lyrics, the 'orchestra' would be primed and ready, the red light would get switched on and off they'd go.

Nowadays people expect, if not demand, rather more involvement than that. Nowadays studios are more complex and option-laden places as well. So much so that some bands have taken years to complete an album, guzzling budgets like telephone numbers along the way. But there's only one thing worse that not having a hit, and that's having a hit and finding that you still owe your record company half a million pounds because you spent so much in the studio.

In the old days making a record was simply one of the many jobs a musician or group had to undertake. It certainly wasn't the be all and end all of life as it is for many people today.

The problem is that as recording equipment has become both more sophisticated and more widely available, everyone today is an expert. Everyone can be an engineer, a producer or an arranger. The result is that musicians get bogged down in the studio; overly involved in recording minutiae that, a handful of years ago, they would not even have known about. And the truth of the matter is that they're wasting their talent, time and money.

Studios, whether demo, MIDI, all-singing, all-dancing mega-track digital, video, or whatever, are places to go into and get out of as quickly and efficiently as possible. Yes, they're fun. Yes, they're an escape. Yes, life outside often ceases to exist. But if you're not careful, they become an end in themselves, and a vantage point from where you can sit and kiss your career – along with any thoughts of a hit record – a fond goodbye.

Studios

1. Demo studios

A demo studio, demo being short for demonstration, is traditionally an inexpensive, down to earth type of studio used for one of two purposes: recording songs to take to record companies in the hope of signing a record deal, or working on new songs before mastering them, once you already have a record deal.

A common problem with demo studios – and working in them – is a collective inability to understand what constitutes a demo. A successful demo is a demo

Modern studio control room equipment is so complex and option-laden that for many musicians, the recording studio has become their entire life instead of just another instrument.

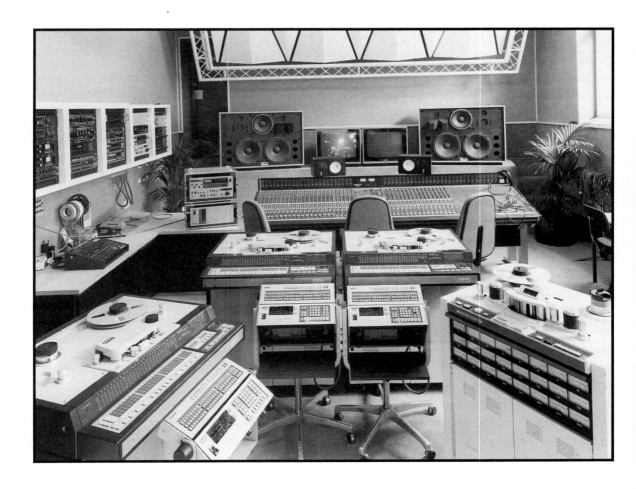

that does one of two things: it gets you signed, or it teaches you how to (or not to) master a song at some later stage.

And that's it. Forget about 'great demos' that *nearly* sound like a finished record – but not quite. What use are they? Record companies find it difficult to get involved when they hear too polished a demo (even though they'll swear this isn't the case) if you're looking for a deal. If you're just working on songs, at best you'll only have to do it all again on the master, and at worst you won't be able to because *recapturing* a brilliant sound or feel is no easy matter.

There are few more frustrating situations than trying, in a £1500 a day top flight studio, to recapture the feel you got on your mate's Portastudio. Except, invariably, failing.

Equipment   Advances in technology keep moving the goalposts when it comes to what you should look for in a demo studio. When the term was first coined in the early '70s, a four-track tape machine, some reverb of sorts and the odd toy like a Roland Space Echo was about as much as you could expect. Two decades later, most operate on 16-track machines, and come laden with every conceivable piece of outboard gear from Japan (the really expensive stuff still tends to be made in the USA or Europe).

Although your budget may prove otherwise, an ideal demo studio would offer the following facilities:

- ● ● ● ● ● ● ● ➤   16-track tape machine
- ● ● ● ● ● ● ● ➤   Sequencing facilities from Atari/Macintosh/Amiga
- ● ● ● ● ● ● ● ➤   SMPTE generation
- ● ● ● ● ● ● ● ➤   Good selection of 'toys' (reverbs, DDLs, limiters etc)
- ● ● ● ● ● ● ● ➤   Digital mastering (Sony F1 or DAT)
- ● ● ● ● ● ● ● ➤   High quality cassette machine
- ● ● ● ● ● ● ● ➤   A 'live' room in addition to the regular control room

Costs   From **£5–10** per hour (8-track) to **£7–20** per hour (16-track)

2. MIDI studios

A MIDI studio is so named because it deals, primarily, in music stored on digital MIDI sequencers as opposed to analogue tape. People use MIDI studios for programming (keyboard and drum machine parts) before going into a regular recording studio, where they can then regurgitate the parts at the press of a button, add guitars, vocals etc, and finally mix.

Why? Because programming can take forever, and a MIDI studio is a) better equipped to deal with programming problems and b) considerably cheaper to hire.

The Fostex R8 eight-track open reel recorder is aimed at home and basic demo studios, although these days, it's common to move straight from four-track cassette to 16-track open reel.

Sometimes a MIDI studio will be sited within or alongside a regular studio. Sometimes it'll be a complete studio in its own right. Many people's home studios are MIDI studios (see *Setting up a home studio on page 82*).

Equipment   A MIDI studio should contain:

● ● ● ● ● ● ● ◗ A good computer-based sequencing package (Steinberg Pro 24/Cubase with Atari ST, MOU Performer with Macintosh etc)
● ● ● ● ● ● ● ◗ High quality sampler (Akai S-1000, Roland S-550)
● ● ● ● ● ● ● ◗ Selection of synths/other keyboards (Roland D-50, Korg M1, Yamaha V-50)
● ● ● ● ● ● ● ◗ Editing software for samplers/synths

Costs   From **£7–20** per hour (though as with all commercial studios, it is normally possible to negotiate lower daily and weekly rates).

3. Master recording studios

This is where your hit will be made. Professional recording studios can be strange and intimidating places with their hi-tech designs, space-station control rooms and personnel who seem only able to speak in jargon.

Itemising equipment, studio costs etc is not necessary here since, unless you're producing your own record without record company/management support, you're neither going to be the one choosing the studio nor (initially) paying the bill.

Understanding what some of the technical terms mean is helpful though.

Bounce: when several tracks are mixed onto a single (or, in stereo, two) tracks. With the increase in 48-track recording you won't need to bounce tracks very often in this situation. Although the activity is also called 'ping ponging' by certain people on the fringes of the business, anyone referring to it thus in a studio would, most likely, be deemed a total prat.

Cans: headphones

Click Track: a metronomic timing track used during the initial stages of recording to preserve 100 per cent timing accuracy for the musicians who're having to put their parts down first. Although the click can be a simple metronome type click, a simple drum machine snare/bass drum pattern is often used as it's marginally less boring to play to.

Digital recording: undoubtedly the recording medium of the future, digital multitracks are still vastly expensive and accordingly, digital recording is always more expensive. Though there are few reasons why not to record digital (other than extra cost), it by no means guarantees a hit. The music is still more important than the medium.

EQ: equalisation — tone controls in layman's terms. Treble is also known as 'top', bass as 'bottom'.

Guide vocal: a rough vocal to both give the instruments something to play to and, more importantly, signposting where not to play (see *Arrangement*, page 89–90).

Monitor mix: a rough mix, with few fancy effects and such, for listening to the track in the studio or, conceivably, taking home and learning from.

Monitors: speakers. Most studios will have a pair of giant speakers the size of a wall, used for detecting microscopic flaws in a sound, along with several other pairs on a more human scale.

Punch-in/out (also known as drop in/out): whereby you replace a certain slice of a track only. Normally you're doing this because you made a mistake at a certain point and being able to drop in and out saves you from having to record the whole part again.

SSL: Solid State Logic — the name of the computer-controlled mixing desk regarded as the best you can buy. Now that so many studios boast SSL desks, however, there's almost a cachet in not having one!

Take: as in 'go for a take' or 'were you taking that?'. Recording.

Setting up a home studio

Home studios can save you from having to hire comnmercial demo or MIDI studios with the added benefits of being a) usable at all hours and b) virtually free once you've set them up. And, seriously, they can enhance your chances of making hit records by:

- Allowing you to write, record, practice etc without having to go out, or having to find large sums of money to finance sessions.
- Earning you money while you keep writing/recording your own material (see book details below).
- Enabling you to learn recording techniques in your own time.
- Making you make a serious commitment to music.

On the downside, a home studio will take over a room (movable home studios, with all the gear stored in cupboards until needed, should be a last resort – you'll never feel like setting it all up), they can cost a fair amount, and you'll find friends dropping in on an almost permanent basis.

Although home studios can be modelled on a MIDI studio, ie based around a sequencer rather than a tape machine, incorporating even something as low-tech as a four-track cassette machine is still advisable. A MIDI studio type won't be much use if you're in an all-guitar band.

The basic machine for any home studio is still the four-track cassette recorder ('Portastudio'). This six-input Tascam Porta Two offers multitracking for just a few hundred pounds.

Home studio buffs often make do with hi-fi speakers for monitoring. But if you're serious, small professional monitors like Yamaha's legendary NS-10Ms can be a worthwhile investment.

The room   In an ideal world you'll want two rooms, adjoining: one to use as a control room, the other for playing, singing, and rehearsing.

Realistically, your money/partner/parents will allow you only one room to play with, though the two-room approach is still viable should that one room be a largish garage or loft (build a stud wall and fill the gap with a horrible [wear gloves] soundproofing material called Rockwool).

Casting ideals aside, let's say you have *a room*. In answer to the question 'do I need to soundproof?', ask your partner or parents, and neighbours. If your music is guitar-based metal thrash, the answer almost certainly is yes. Andreas Vollenweider? Maybe you'll get away with it.

Soundproofing the floor, ceiling, walls, and doors is expensive. If you do anything at all it's more likely to be to *reduce* rather than eliminate the noise. Something is better than nothing, though, since continually being told to turn down/off can become a real turn-off for your creative juices.

Low cost ways to cut down noise include:

- Eggboxes on ceiling (horrible but effective)
- Plenty of cushions/drapes around the place
- Clingfilm-type double glazing
- Carpets (off-cuts?) on walls and doors
- Double carpet on floor

With all the above you may forget two other important factors: light, and air. Don't. You need plenty of both to avoid brain-damage after a while!

The equipment For all the forests worth of magazines, books, and assorted literature on the subject of recording gear, it's still a fair bet that no two people own identical home recording set-ups. There is, in other words, no perfect system.

You want to make hit records, don't you? You don't want to become a recording engineer, or worse, a boffin. But if you're going to launch your career from home, like a Howard Jones or Paul Hardcastle, or maintain it from home as almost all writers do today, then sooner or later you're going to have learn a little about recording equipment and recording techniques.

There are four categories of equipment to bear in mind for your system:

1   **Instruments** (guitars, keyboards, drum machines, mikes)

2   **Digital controlling devices** (sequencer, computer, sync/MIDI devices)

3   **Recorders/mixers** (multitracks, mastering equipment)

4   **Outboard** (signal processors, reverbs, DDLs)

1. INSTRUMENTS

Of course you use what you use, yes? But if you're going to the trouble of setting up a home studio, think carefully about how your current equipment fits into your intended scheme. If it doesn't (you've got loads of old, non MIDI synths, non MIDI drum machine etc), then it's worth trading in for something more applicable.

A perfect home studio would contain:

Acoustic guitar
Electric guitar(s) (amps)
Drum machine
Acoustic drums
Digital synth(s)
Analogue synth(s)
Sampler
Acoustic piano/digital piano
Selection of mikes

Please see the relevant sections for notes on the above instrument types. A microphone? Well, aside from their voices, the nearest thing singers have to bits of gear is a mike. And seeing as how what will sell you material more than anything else will be the lead vocal, don't skimp on mikes. Read up on the subject, and talk to users, before buying.

● Wind and guitar players can easily get in on the MIDI act these days using a MIDI wind controller, or a MIDI guitar, to control synths/samplers/digital pianos and/or input data into sequencers.

2. DIGITAL CONTROLLING DEVICES
(See also sequencers, page 57)

If you're a keyboard player a sequencer will probably be at the heart of your system. The relative merits of dedicated sequencers and sequencing software are discussed on page 58, but in a home studio setting, two additional factors come into play. A dedicated sequencer takes up less room, but a personal computer can also be used to run programs for storing instrument patches, and can help with mixing and solving MIDI muddles.

Speaking of which, although MIDI is no longer the fraught 'will it work or won't it?' business it used to be, sundry MIDI 'boxes' remain essential for most home studios. The first is a box to organise and streamline MIDI data. A simple MIDI Thru box (1 or 2 Ins, 4 or more Thrus) may suffice if you're not using many instruments. On the other hand devices like the Sycologic M16 or the

Digital Music Corp MX-8 (that enable you to program and store lots of MIDI routings) can save hours of fiddling about and repatching.

The further up the high tech ladder you climb, the more important some form of 'synching' (synchronisation) system becomes. Here's why.

You own a sequencer, a drum machine, a guitar and a four-track cassette machine. You get a nice drum track going ... you program a nice little bass line into the sequencer... you record it on the four-track. You play some guitar over the top. Then you think of a really catchy little riffy synth part. You're stuck. How can you get the sequencer to play 'in sync' with what's already on tape? Without a synching system you can't.

MIDI has a built-in synching system enabling, say, a MIDI-linked sequencer and drum machine to play perfectly in time with each other. But that's no help for synching instruments to tape. In practice, your choice consists of:

FSK or Frequency Shift Keying low tech, inexpensive, a little out of date. You'll need a MIDI convertor such as Yamaha's YMC10.

SMPTE the modern approach. 'Striping', as they say, your tape with SMPTE (which stands for the Society of Motion Picture & Television Engineers, whose timecode for film and TV synchronisation it is) opens the door for recordings made at home to be usable in even the most up-to-the-mark and hip studio. SMPTE generators are no longer fiercely priced, and the investment is well worth it.

3. RECORDERS/MIXERS

It may seem like the whole world's gone digital these days, but for the foreseable future, you'll still be needing good old analogue tape machines somewhere in your home studio.

Sequencers are great but they won't record guitar parts or vocals. For these,

and other purposes, what you need is a multitrack recorder – and unless you're filthy rich (in which case you can simply buy yourself a hit record!) you'll be looking at analogue, tape-based machines, from four-track cassettes (Portastudio being the Tascam product name widely adopted as a generic term for these beasts) to open-reel 16-tracks.

Four-track cassettes The choice is vast. There's even a couple of eight-track cassettes. As always, you get what you pay for. Useful features to ask about include:

Simultaneous four-track recording (some record only two tracks at a time)
Two or more effects busses
Dual speed
'Zero return'
Dolby 'C' or dbx noise reduction

Quality varies from machine to machine, but with four tracks of music crammed onto so narrow a band as cassette tape,you're not going to get, in pure audio terms at any rate, professional results; all the less if you persist in 'bouncing' too many tracks together. With careful recording, however, and sensible use of sequencers (you shouldn't *need* to commit sequenced parts to tape; just route them, via your mixer, straight to your mastering device) you can still get perfectly good results.

On the other hand you may want to look at:

Open reel multitracks Don't even contemplate such systems unless you really want to learn about recording. The recorders are expensive, you'll need more ancillary gear, and the whole process of recording is fairly complex. The gap between being able to understand a four-track cassette and eight/16-track open reel is far wider than from an eight/16-track system to a £1,500-a-day mastering studio.

But the advantages are many: generally, the machines are made to a higher audio specification than cassette systems; you'll *have* to have a good quality dedi-

Advances in technology have now made eight-track cassette recorders such as the Toa MR-8T viable. For the home studio, they offer cassette convenience *and* multitrack flexibility.

cated mixer; there are more tracks to play with. It should all add up to better quality recordings – more professional, more saleable.

Partly due to the complexity factor, many people find that eight-track systems are a bit of a waste of time. The thinking is that if you've got to do a substantial amount of head-scratching anyway, you might as well have a system that is a substantial improvement over the cassettes.

If you're thinking of moving up to, or indeed starting off with, one of these systems, you should seek advice from a specialist shop or at the very least consult one of the books listed below dedicated to the subject.

The tape machine and mixer alone will probably cost £5,000, with more expense, invariably, to come. Fostex and Tascam make the most popular tape machines, though Akai has a number of integrated recorder/mixer packages using a special 'video tape' type format which have proved popular.

Mixers Mixers look absurdly complicated. In reality they're not, for the simple reason that although most seem as if they have a thousand different knobs and switches on them, the knobs and switches run in vertical lines, or 'channels', each channel being identical to its neighbour. Learn what one channel does and you have learned 90 per cent of the mixer.

Multitrack tape machines operate as four, eight, 16, 24, or 48 *track* devices; mixers offer four, eight, 16 etc *channels*, each channel controlling the volume, pan position, and certain tonal characteristics of a track. As a rule of thumb you should buy a mixer that has twice the number of channels as your tape machine has tracks.

Although a separate mixer is not compulsory when using a four-track cassette – since all have their own built in – a mixer *will* be necessary for open reel recorders, which, normally, are recording machines only.

Mastering Master is the term used to describe a finished recording, whether it

Multi-channel desks like this Yamaha 2800M look daunting until you realise that each column of controls is identical for all 40 channels. Using it is not likely to be *your* problem anyway!

be simply ready to play at home on a cassette, or ready to be cut into a commercial record.

To obtain a master recording you must mix all the tracks on your multitrack down onto just two tracks, left and right, ie stereo.

For years there was no argument about the format of machine you should use for mastering. You mastered onto ¼inch tape, the most famous machine (even though it's not been used in pro studios for ages) being the Revox by Studer.

For home studios a Revox can still be a good idea; the machines are high quality, not too expensive (though being Swiss made, not cheap either), and you can easily edit the tape using the low cost tools of an editing board, chinagraph pencil and clean razor blade. Along with plenty of courage!

But as most finished demos are listened to on cassette, many people prefer to buy a high quality cassette recorder to master on in the first place. While perfectly acceptable sound-wise (moreover you won't lose a generation of tape by otherwise having to copy from quarter inch to cassette) you will, however, forego any editing facilities.

Digital mastering, if not digital recording, is almost standard practice in recording studios. The advantages, sound-wise, are considerable: unlimited copies with no sound degradation, no hiss, no coloration etc. Even for home studios, the cost of digital mastering is not excessive.

As of writing, the most common format remains Betamax tape on one of the Sony range of recorders, usually the F1. But DAT, accepted as providing even higher quality results, is only just around the corner now that the machines themselves are becoming more widely available. The only drawback with either format is that editing, as yet, is expensive and/or difficult.

Costs Sony F1: **£1,190** (now discontinued); Sony PCM 701: **£979**; Casio DA-1/2 around **£700**

4. OUTBOARD

Outboard gear, 'toys', signal processors, call them what you will, all add life to your recordings, and will help home-recorded tracks sound as if they've been recorded in a regular commercial studio.

There are various types of device, from dramatic, sound enhancing 'effects' like DDLs and reverb, to seemingly more mundane gadgets such as limiters, noise gates, and equalisers. Most outboard equipment comes in module form, designed to slot into a (standard) 19 inch rack.

Reverb makes recordings sound professional. Simple as that. Without reverb, most recordings tend to sound a little flat, a little dull, a little unexciting. Keyboards and vocals are both frequently enhanced by DDLs (Digital Delay Lines), whose 'effect' ranges from quasi double-tracking (a sound thickening effect) to endless echoes.

Although dedicated devices will deliver the highest quality results, multi-effects processors are now all the rage. Most of the major companies produce modules which, variously, combine DDL, reverb, EQ, and limiting facilities – notably the Quadraverb from the American company Alesis, which can perform up to four such tasks simultaneously.

Setting up a home studio cannot guarantee you a hit of course, but it will guarantee you a lot of fun in the process.

Books on recording include:

Making 4-Track Music, John Peel (Track Record)
Recording Production Techniques for Musicians, Bruce Nazarian (Amsco)
Home Recording for Musicians, Craig Anderton (Amsco)
The Home Recording Handbook, Chris Everard (Virgin)

Personal Recording (Hal Leonard/Yamaha Foundation)
The MIDI Home Studio, Howard Massey (Amsco)
How To Make Money From Home Recording, Clive Brooks (PC Publishing)
The Digital Delay Handbook, Craig Anderton (Amsco)

Recording courses are also run at:

Gateway School of Recording & Music Technology
Salford College of Technology, Manchester

City University, London
Goldsmiths College, London
School of Audio Engineering, Manchester
University of Surrey, Guildford

CHAPTER
EIGHT

RECORDING –
'THE ART'

● ▶ ● ▶ ● ▶ *All dressed up and nowhere to go?*

Arrangements
and routining

The word arrangement might sound a bit posey, or a bit classical, but it is simply a term used to describe the process of figuring out which bit comes where in a song, and what instrument plays it.

Some people can arrange their own songs, some rely on producers, others hire arrangers.

One thing is certain, though, and that is that the arrangement is vital to the success of your record.

In the old days 'artistes' would simply turn up at the studio and sing over an arrangement, written by an arranger and played, most likely, by a small orchestra. When groups first appeared – populated by people who could actually play their own musical instruments – the arranger's role was split in two: said arranger was now confined to writing string or brass arrangements, while someone else, normally the producer, 'routined' the basic structure of the song with the group.

This situation remains today; the distinctions between routining and arranging, and now production, being just a little more blurred.

But it really doesn't matter what you call it, what matters is that your song is recorded in such a way – dressed up if you like – as to make it as irresistible as possible to the record-buying public.

Recognising arrangement/routining/production skills is a lot easier than being able to say, precisely, what it is that makes a great arrangement.

Or is it?

Hum any hit single – start to finish. The chances are you'll be humming an instrumental intro, followed by a little drum fill into the first verse, then the vocal, that little bass turnaround in the middle, the lead into the chorus, the vocals, the brass stabs . . .

In other words there is no dead space. *Something* that catches your ear is happening all the time.

This shouldn't be taken to mean that you've got to cram supposedly 'catchy' lines into every nanosecond of recording – a groove, or even space, can be quite sufficient for many a bar – but the mind should never be allowed to wander and start thinking about something else like the supper, the weather or the time.

This is precisely what's happening when a record company executive presses fast forward when listening to your tape. It's what happens when Radio 1 is passing on your record for the playlist. It's what happens when the record doesn't become a hit.

There are degrees of 'ear-catchingness' of course. Not every successful record appears brilliantly arresting the first time you hear it. Some records are 'sleepers' or growers. But if you submit your arrangement to the 'hum' test (is there something you can hum all the way through?), you probably won't be far wrong.

The skill comes in arriving at such an arrangement without the seams showing. 'Catchiness' can sometimes be too contrived.

To this end, although talk of arrangements doesn't usually start until you get to the demo stage, if, when you're writing a song, you feel or 'hear' a catchy drum fill, bass line or brass barp, REMEMBER IT. Write it down. The chances are that such naturally arrived-at parts will be worth remembering.

There's only one thing worse than having no catchy parts to listen to. And that's having two or more catchy parts to listen to at the same time. This is the oldest arrangement trap to fall into, especially for bands.

Here's what happens. The bass player finds this neat catchy link between vocal lines in the verse. Mmm, thinks the guitarist, I like that; this riff'll just fit in nicely with it.

The drummer hears what's happening and slots in a fill; the keyboard player doubles what the bass player's doing. Before you know where you are there's a battle going on.

Any one of the parts would be great. BUT NOT ALL AT THE SAME TIME. If you want to play jazz, and spend a life being admired and broke, fine. You want a hit record? Sort out who's playing what, where, and don't tread on each others toes. The pop record-buying ear only likes assimilating one 'line' at a time.

Sounds

In the same way that a fill, run, or turnaround can help your cause, a different sound – a weird effect on a guitar, a particular type of echo on the voice, a heavily processed tom sound – is often the thing that grabs people's attention. While not every hit has its own distinctive sound in there somewhere, a remarkable number have.

Stock, Aitken and Waterman could do no wrong in the late '80s – they even turned Australian soap actors into international artistes.

Basic song structure

Intro/Chorus – Verse 1 – Chorus – Verse 2 – Chorus – Breakdown/Middle 8 – Chorus – Chorus – Chorus – Fade/End. This, with minor deviations like Verse 2 running on from Verse 1, and there being a third verse after the middle section, is how most hit records are structured.

There will always be exceptions – John Miles' 'Music', Richard Harris' 'MacArthur's Park'. They simply prove the rule.

The key

The authors are not aware of any research showing the key of E to have any magical hitmaking properties, but it's a fair bet that this, the most common 'guitar' key, has appeared on more hit records than most. For the same reason, the key of A is very popular, followed by D . . .

Keyboard-playing songwriters tend to write in flat keys (B flat, E flat, A flat especially), and both A minor and D minor are evocative, tear jerking sorts of keys ideal for the mawkish ballad.

Time signature

This is easier. Country music artists seem to be able to get away with waltz time 3/4 or 6/8 time signatures but for the vast majority of rock and pop hits, it's 4/4 all the way, a fact that explains, in a few brief words, why Frank Zappa makes great records, but not *hit* records.

BPM

This stands for Beats Per Minute. It is said that 120 bpm *is* the magic 'gets 'em all onto the dance floor' tempo ('I heard It Through The Grapevine' being a classic example, though Chic's 'Le Freak' is a shade faster at 122). But groove, and the song's ability to suck the listener in, are far more important factors.

Throughout the history of pop, there's always been a demand for records you can smooch to on the dance floor (for pretty damn obvious reasons), which run at much slower bpms than this. At the top end, demonic thrashes have been hits also, though a tempo beyond 135 bpm would be undanceable-to for all but the most demented of speedfreaks.

Duration

The perfect single is no longer than 3 minutes 30 seconds says Radio 1; this, presumably, being the researched attention span of the average pop listener. Make singles any longer, and at best, your track will be faded out after 3:30 or, at worst, your record will be deemed 'too long' and shunned.

Again, exceptions there are, which only prove the rule.

One of the cardinal rules of hitmaking is: stick to simple 4/4 time signatures. Frank Zappa is renowned for not doing so, which is why he makes *great* records but not *hit* records.

From his Buggles days, Trevor Horne (left) went on to become one of the most sought-after producers following successes like Frankie Goes To Hollywood. But a big name doesn't guarantee a hit.

Except, of course, 12inch singles. Records mixed or re-mixed for the dance floor are a law unto themselves time-wise. In other arrangement terms, 12inches are different from regular singles in that their overriding purpose is to be danceable, to provide an incessant and unswerving beat.

Although the best 12inches still manage to stimulate what's left of one's brain at two in the morning on a hot 'n' sweaty dancefloor, repetition and 'anything goes' samples are their stock in trade.

Arrangement tips

- No dead space. Something 'interesting' must be happening at all times.
- Use a different, stimulating sound or effect on an instrument/vocal.
- Stick to classic structures, time signatures, and timings.
- Don't clutter.
- Allow each 'catchy' part its own space.

Books on arranging include:

Arranging Concepts Complete, Dick Grover (Alfred)

The Contemporary Arranger, Don Sebesky (Alfred)

Making demos

As mentioned in Chapter 7, there are two reasons why people make demos: to sell themselves or the song to a record company or publisher, or to test-record a song once they already have a deal.

If you are in the former category, you will understand more about what makes a *good* demo by putting yourself in the latter category for a moment.

So you've demoed up a dozen songs or more for your next album . . . you've got to do some weeding out. That song you spent weeks on; it sounds sort of clogged up now, doesn't it? And that last one – the one that only took half a day to write and finish. It sounds great: simple, fresh . . .

There's an art to making demos, and essentially that art is to keep the recording as simple, fresh, and up-front as possible. If you spent days or weeks poring over the *demo* of a song, you run the risk of becoming bored before you even get to mastering it.

A good demo should make the outside listener want to hear more. A good demo should have *you* straining at the leash to get back in the studio to record it for real.

Now this is all very well in theory. In practice, although you go in with the best of intentions, somehow you find yourself getting carried away with *perfecting* that solo, working out the precise, mathematically correct repeat on that vocal etc.

Ways to avoid that clogged-up feeling

●●●●●●● ▶ Get in a producer, even if it's someone relatively inexperienced.

●●●●●●● ▶ Set a limit of, say, one day/half day per song. And stick to it.

●●●●●●● ▶ Limit the number of tracks you use.

●●●●●●● ▶ Record in such a way that at least part of the demo can be used on a master recording.

This last solution involves a little planning, no more. If it's analogue parts you feel you'll want to keep (vocal parts, guitar parts), then you must ensure the tape you make the demo on is time-coded with SMPTE so that it can be locked in with another tape machine later on. If the parts are digital (drum machine, keyboard etc), then you will be able to transfer a demo-initiated sequence onto a master tape without any problems at all.

Creativity

If everything you record on a demo – parts, songs, approaches, arrangements – works, you'd better hope you can transfer most of it onto the master! Demos are for taking risks, embarking on outlandish concepts, failing gloriously. DON'T PLAY SAFE ON DEMOS.

Things you should learn about the song from its demo

● ● ● ● ● ● ● ▶   Key

● ● ● ● ● ● ● ▶   Tempo

● ● ● ● ● ● ● ▶   Basic song structure

● ● ● ● ● ● ● ▶   Feel

● ● ● ● ● ● ● ▶   Instrumentation (roughly)

● ● ● ● ● ● ● ▶   Whether it'll need non-band instruments like strings or brass

What you don't need to settle upon

● ● ● ● ● ● ● ▶   The finished solo (if there is one)

● ● ● ● ● ● ● ▶   Exact instrumentation (and sounds of)

● ● ● ● ● ● ● ▶   Effects

A demo is, after all, a recording, so many of the principles and golden rules are the same as those listed in the *Mastering – Life In The Studio* section which follows.

Mastering –
life in the studio

This is it. This is the moment you've been waiting for, for weeks, months, years?

This is also the moment that sorts out the men from the boys or the women from the girls. A tiny proportion of artists who try to get signed get signed. A pretty small proportion of those who do get signed get successful. And the reason – although most who don't succeed will prefer to blame the record company, the management, the promotion budget etc – is that they haven't made the right type of records.

It's useless talking about records that weren't 'good' enough or 'commercial' enough. What is good? And commerciality can only be judged in retrospect.

If a record doesn't sell, there's something wrong; and the chances are it'll be that the record wasn't right for its market, or that there wasn't a market for such a record in the first place. Conversely you don't need a six figure promotional budget to have a hit. Hits can just happen.

Dire Straits' 'Sultans Of Swing' (the record that broke the band) is a classic case in point. The band's American record company were sufficiently unimpressed that they weren't even going to release the record, and it was only a pestering secretary who persuaded them otherwise. There was no promotional budget to speak of, no fuss at all.

Record label bosses don't always spot the winners. 'Sultans Of Swing', which put Dire Straits on the map, was released by their US label only following a secretary's continual pestering.

But radio stations got to hear of it, loved it, played the song to death, and the public bought it in droves. It was a perfect record for its time.

What's all this got to do with life in the studio? Attitude, mainly.

It's in the studio that you're talked into fat, multi-layered guitar sounds simply because 'then it'll be perfect for America' and not because that's what you want. It's in the studio that you spend hours making sure everything is 'perfect', frequently so perfect that the result ceases to sound human. It's in the studio that you clam up, get nervous, and play safe. It's in the studio that you try so hard to put in as many 'catchy' lines as you can that the song suffocates.

Now some of these problems should be avoided or solved by the producer. But ultimately it's your record. It's your attitude towards recording and making music that will stamp itself on what you record – and govern, to a very large extent, whether or not you've made a hit.

The attitude you *need* has got nothing to do with musical style or personality (one artist may spend a week recording, another a year; one might like trashing the place at the end of the evening, another playing chess) rather it can be described, quite simply, as honesty.

The public can spot a phoney better than you think. Really successful horrible, crass, 'commercial' records are invariably made by those who really *love* horrible, crass, 'commercial' music.

Provided you can hold on to what you believe in, and don't get blown off course by friends' comments, or by last-minute pressure from eager A&R men, the process of recording your master is up to you and your producer. No single system works better than any other. However . . .

Some of the things that'll make life easier in the studio

● ● ● ● ● ● ● ➤ Eating properly

● ● ● ● ● ● ● ➤ Taking regular breaks, getting some fresh air

● ● ● ● ● ● ● ➤ Wearing loose, comfortable clothes

● ● ● ● ● ● ● ➤ Treating the engineer with respect

● ● ● ● ● ● ● ➤ A sense of humour (though not at each other's expense)

● ● ● ● ● ● ● ➤ Knowing when to quit. If a take's not going well after a while, take a break. Move on

Things that'll make life worse

● ● ● ● ● ● ● ➤ Excessive smoking, boozing, or partaking of any mind-altering substances

● ● ● ● ● ● ● ➤ Too much coffee (try drinking hot water after a time, you won't notice the difference – honest!)

● ● ● ● ● ● ● ➤ Friends dropping in

● ● ● ● ● ● ● ➤ Instruments breaking down/discovering you don't have any spare guitar strings/drum sticks etc

● ● ● ● ● ● ● ➤ Paying too much attention to what 'outsiders' think (do that beforehand, it's too late now)

● ● ● ● ● ● ● ➤ Laughing at fellow band members' mistakes

George Martin (right) became famous as The Beatles' producer with albums like 'Sgt Pepper'. But those same tracks *un*mixed prove just how good was the basic material he had to work with.

Producers

A myth, carefully cultivated by producers and one aided and abetted by spiralling instrument technology, is that producers make or break records.

They can. They have. But what makes or breaks a record is the song and your peformance of it – two things in which the vast majority of producers have no special skill nor involvement.

But still producers can command telephone number advances, more 'points' than any single band member and industry adulation beyond their wildest deserts.

Part of the problem is that producers have no clearly defined job description. Engineers must twiddle knobs in order to become engineers, singers must sing, drummers drum.

Producers produce. Yes, but what? The title of producer covers a whole range of involvements, from those who'll roost in large, comfy armchairs, occasionally looking up to say that it sounds good to them and isn't it time for lunch, to those who'll grill you on the meaning of every lyric, tell you when to breathe, how to hold your pick, will re-write the song, and probably record it too, given half the chance.

The trick is telling one from t'other and knowing which'll suit you the best.

The first thing not to be swayed by is 'name'.

Record companies love names. 'We'd like you to work with Arnie Schmuck; you know, he produced the Flying A&R Men who had that massive hit 'Dead From The Neck Upwards' last summer . . .'

Oh did he? So what's to say that Arnie's involvement had anything to do with their success? Of course you can't prove it either way. But what you can say is that just because your chosen producer had a massive hit with someone else, it doesn't mean he's going to have a massive hit with you. Or, more's the point, that if he does have a massive hit with you it's because of him that you've had it!

Pressed on the point, record companies may even admit to this. But they'll still come back with arguments like 'it'll make the radio stations take notice'.

This, too, is arrant nonsense. 'Hey, this record really sucks but . . . look, it was produced by Arnie Schmuck . . . it's a hit. Play it!'

So if it's not status, what should you choose your producer on?

On compatibility – musically and personally – ie meet the person first. On expertise – you know they're a keyboard whizz, vocalist, engineer . . . On instinct.

Do you feel that your intended producer is up for the job because he sincerely likes your material, because the head of A&R is an old mate, because they badly need the money, bread and butter job – a fill in? Instinct will have to suffice as to whether you're right.

Having chosen a producer, he'll be the one in charge once you're in the studio. Unless you like working with a dictator, this shouldn't mean that every decision goes his way – and no arguments – but equally, if you're paying someone to give your record a direction, not following their suggestions is rather a waste of everyone's energy.

The mix

You may or may not be directly involved with the mix (where what's been recorded on a multitrack recorder is 'mixed' down into stereo, adding effects, EQ, parts fading in and out etc), depending upon you and/or your producer.

The mix is where your song is snipped, tucked, pushed and polished into the finished article. It is also, special 12inch remixes aside, not the be all and end all of the record.

If what you've recorded sounds pretty ropey, you'll soon discover the fallacy of the phrase 'we can fix that in the mix', because the chances are you can't.

All too often it's the mix that's blamed for a song's lack of hit potential (which is why an artist can be sent back to remix it over and over again, or new blood brought in to have a go) when the real fault lies in the song, or in its performance.

To credit, as some must do, the listening public with ears that can detect a marginally too trebly tambourine or a snare drum that has the punch only of a Joe Frazier, not a Mike Tyson, is absurd.

If you've recorded the song sympathetically — and sympathetically to your image and ability — then, within reason, the mix is unlikely to have any real effect on whether it becomes a hit or not.

Classic confirmation could be found a few years ago when a West End music shop acquired one of Abbey Road's four-track machines along with the (four-track) tape of The Beatles' 'Sgt Pepper' album. No matter how you re-mixed the tracks, it still sounded, well, like it sounds! The commerciality lay in the songs, the arrangements, the performances, and in the basic recording.

RELEASING
YOUR OWN RECORD

●▶●▶●▶ *The DIY way to hike up your credibility*

EVERYBODY can't get a record deal, but anybody can put out a record.

There are two main reasons artists or bands press up their own records. Vanity is the first. The second is the desire to be taken seriously by fans/the press/the music business generally.

The latter is obviously an avenue worthy of exploration by the aspiring hitmaker. Having your music on vinyl – albeit on your own 'one off' label – is an indisputable hike in your credibility.

It means you're committed. And it means your music is far more likely to be listened to – by the music papers, who may review it; by distributors, who may agree to take it on and get it into record stores; and by management companies, publishers and record companies, who may give you more consideration as a potential new signing.

So making your own record is an important way of promoting your career – and who knows, you may even sell enough copies to make a profit as well!

Starting your
own label

Starting a label is a lot simpler than it sounds. All you have to do is say I have started a label, and it is called XYZ . . . And when your record comes out with 'XYZ' on it, that's proof enough that the label exists.

You don't have to form a limited company; you don't need to register the name; you don't even need to have headed notepaper – although all these things may be desirable at a later stage if your label develops into a going concern rather than simply existing for the life of one record.

If you're in a band, your label could be an equal partnership of all members, the name of the label being the name under which the partnership 'trades'. Or it could be a partnership of the songwriting team within the band. Or it could be a

partnership with the person who puts up the money to press your record! A partnership costs you nothing.

A limited company, on the other hand, costs about £125 to set up and must be properly constituted under company law, return annual accounts, be audited and so on. At this level, there's not much point in going to that amount of trouble.

So all you have to do is decide on a label name and you've got yourself a label. Of course, if you decide to call it CBS or EMI, you might find it has an even shorter life than you anticipated – not to mention considerably higher costs – so check first that someone else isn't already using the name. The annual *Music Business Directory* lists record labels.

Pressing your own records is usually done primarily for promotional purposes. But some bands like the Sperm Wails have had commercial success with self-pressed product.

Vinyl solutions

The same directory also lists hundreds of record pressing operations, printers and tape duplicators. So how do you decide who to go to, and what is it exactly that you need?

The elements that you need to take care of in order to end up with something that resembles a record bought in a record store are as follows:

- ●●●●●●●▶ A stereo master recording, usually from your demo session, and on $\frac{1}{4}$ inch tape, but also acceptable in the form of a home-mastered stereo cassette, DAT cassette or Sony digital cassette.
- ●●●●●●●▶ Lacquers, cut from the tape supplied. These are the two master discs used to press both sides of your vinyl offering.
- ●●●●●●●▶ The pressings themselves.
- ●●●●●●●▶ Labels for both sides of each disc.
- ●●●●●●●▶ Packaging for the discs.

A glance at the *Music Week Directory* quickly confirms that there are literally hundreds of companies providing the necessary services. So shopping around is going to be the best way to ensure your own ideal combination of cutting, pressing and printing. If you have the energy.

Excessive time, large phone bills and possibly, ultimate disappointment can be avoided, however, if you ask around first. Just like recording studios, cutting studios have reputations, and if you can find one that comes recommended and offers what you need at the right price, you'll often find that the rest of the chain falls into place, because the cutting studio will be able to recommend pressing companies and the pressing companies will be able to recommend printers.

Cutting

When you go to a cutting studio, you'll usually find there are two rates – attended and unattended. The unattended rate will be cheaper, because it means the studio can slot your job in at a time convenient to them – like 3 o'clock in the morning – and just get on with the job, instead of having to go to the trouble of arranging a time that's also convenient to you.

However, this is generally reckoned to be a false economy. Old hands agree that whatever other stages you leave to other people, there's one thing you should always do.

Always be in on the cut.

Why? Because it gives you the opportunity to make last-minute improvements to the sound of your music. You have a chance to influence how loud the cut will be, how it's equalised (more bass, less mid or whatever), the amount of compression etc. And if your recording has been done somewhat on the cheap

Old hands at the DIY record game say you should always be "in on the cut" since even at this stage, there's much you can do to 'tweak' the quality of your finished product.

(which is usually the case), the facility for these kind of last-minute improvements can make all the difference to how good your music sounds 'under the needle'.

Some cutting studios work on an hourly rate. Since an hourly rate can be £100–150, you could find yourself lumbered with an unexpectedly hefty cutting bill, especially if your presence at the cut means that the job takes four hours instead of one! But there are studios who'll cut a seven-inch for a fixed price (typically around £100) so this obviously represents a better deal, especially if you intend to take some time getting everything right.

Artwork

Origination of artwork for your labels and sleeves can be a very costly business if you pay a printer or professional studio to do it. But since the chances are that either someone in your band or someone close to it will be artistically inclined, this is one of the jobs you can take on yourselves.

Artwork can be produced in line (solid) or tone (shades), in one colour (ie black on white) or as many as four (which is full colour printing). You could have an artist friend draw your label and sleeve art, or you could use Letraset – or even a typewriter if all you want on the label/sleeve is lettering.

If you want professional typesetting but nothing much else, it probably will be most economical to give the work to the the same company that is printing your labels and sleeves. But check whether they do their own typesetting or farm it out; if the latter, you might find that a local typesetter is cheaper/more convenient.

Remember, the key phrase here is 'camera-ready'. That means that your finished artwork is in a form that can, if necessary, be reduced (preferable) or enlarged (not so good) to the exact size and shape of the label/sleeve, and of a quality that will photograph properly. If you're not sure, explain what your intentions are and you'll soon be told whether the finished results will qualify as 'camera-ready'.

But while shopping around is definitely the cheapest way to make a record – *if* you know what you're shopping for – you may not have either the time or inclination for learning the ins and outs of a business like printing, just so you can talk authoritatively about choice of fonts and cost of half-tones. In which case, another solution is the package deal. There are a number of companies who will offer to do everything for you, handling not only the cutting of your lacquers and the pressing of your vinyl but also the origination and printing of labels and sleeves.

Be careful.

Package deals

In theory, going to one company who'll do the lot should mean savings all round, but it often doesn't. Most companies who offer package deals don't actually do all the work themselves but simply co-ordinate the various elements, for which you will obviously pay a handling charge. You might be quite happy with their services if what you want happens to fit with the way they like to do things. But ask for anything out of the ordinary and you may encounter problems.

Be especially careful if you go to one of the really big companies. They may claim to offer a personal service, and you may be seduced by the fact that they're handling work for major names and major labels alongside your little job. But face it, who do you think is going to get priority? Your one-off thousand pressings or Megabuck Records' monthly 100,000? Quite.

Costs

By shopping around, you ought to be able to press-up a thousand seven-inch singles from your $\frac{1}{4}$inch master tape, get professionally originated two-colour artwork for labels and single colour artwork for sleeves plus have labels and sleeves printed for around £850 at time of writing.

For a typical package deal, costs might break down as follows:

Basic charge for mastering from a $\frac{1}{4}$ inch tape (reducing to £120 if you provide the lacquers) **£195**

Pressing 1,000 seven-inches at 23p per copy **£230**

Printing, 1,000 inserts at 7p per insert **£70**

Printers' platemaking **£25**

Minimum cost for printing 1,000 simple 2 colour sleeves **£400**

Total: **£895**

Being satisfied with just the plain white bags included in the pressing charge will bring basic pressing cost down to around £500 a saving of almost half.

And what if your first run sells out and you need a second pressing? You can reduce the cost somewhat by advance planning.

Obviously you'll already have your lacquers, so you won't have to pay for those again. But remember: if it costs £70 to print 1,000 labels, it probably costs only £80 or £90 to print 2,000. So for an extra £10–20, you can equip yourself very cheaply, in advance, with labels for your anticipated second pressing too.

Cassette pets

You may want to consider the option of releasing a cassette rather than a single. This is particularly popular on the indie scene as a means for small bands to put out an album or EP of their music at minimum cost.

But it does not have the same *cachet* as putting your music on vinyl.

Despite the popularity of pre-recorded commercial tapes in this era of the Walkman, a cassette as a 'sole product' still has an aura of the home-made, the amateur, the *demo* about it. From a self-promotion point of view, vinyl still equates with 'professional', and the size and shape of a record sleeve provide a far superior medium for conveying your image.

The indie approach to tapes usually means selling them at gigs or through mail-order advertisements in the music press.

The advantage of this approach for most bands is that you gear your expenditure directly to your sales – ie, before a gig, you run off just as many tapes at home as you expect to sell that night, and with mail order sales you run off tapes only as and when you get people's cheques or postal orders through the letterbox.

But doing it this way, you naturally lose the economies of scale obtained by financing a run of, say, a thousand at a professional duplication house.

Duplication

costs

Suppose you decide to issue the cassette equivalent of our hypothetical DIY single – a thousand C10 tapes. This is roughly what it would cost you using a typical tape duplication service – Accurate Sound, based in Leicester – if you supplied them with a master on $\frac{1}{4}$ inch tape, digital or DAT:

Mastering charge (one-off)	**£35**
1,000 C10s at 25p per cassette	**£250**
1,000 cassette cases at 6p per case	**£60**
Origination of insert artwork (typical cost)	**£50**
Printers' platemaking	**£25**
Printing 1,000 inserts at 7p per insert	**£70**
Labels: platemaking from camera-ready artwork	**£25**
Printing and affixing 1,000 label pairs at 3p per pair	**£30**
Total:	**£545**

Costs are based on ordinary ferric cassette tape. Chrome tape is slighly more expensive. But you could save £10 by having 'on body' printing for your cassette labelling (the words printed directly onto the plastic) – this costs only 2p per unit.

Cutting compact discs at Mayking Records' French associate company. Mayking is probably the best known of the UK firms offering a complete DIY service, including in-house graphics.

Compact disc and CDV

If vinyl makes you look professional, then CD also adds to that an impression of exclusivity. From a promotional (and sales) viewpoint, a CD product undoubtedly enjoys higher status.

Of course, if you're thinking of self-releasing a CD 'single' (the 3 inch format carries space for 20 minutes of music), it is worth planning for it by making sure that your stuff has been at least digitally mastered (even small studios have Sony F1 or DAT mastering facilities these days), if not digitally recorded. But if you want CDs made from your $\frac{1}{4}$inch analogue master tape, you can have them.

Costs

If you went to Mayking Records, who are major manufacturers of CD and CDV as well as vinyl, a thousand 3inch CD singles in slimline cases complete with labels and inserts would cost you around **£1,500**.

CDV – compact disc video – is a relatively new medium which has not yet established much of a market in Britain. But it does represent an exciting audio-visual opportunity for anyone with the necessary funds. You can put up to six minutes of promo video *and* 20 minutes of audio on a 5inch disc. Cost is around half as much again as a CD single.

Distribution

Okay, you've got your thousand singles, CDs or whatever stacked up in boxes in the garage – now what are you going to do with them?

You may have earmarked a large proportion of them as promotional giveaways.

But even after you've mailed one to every record label, every publisher, every management company and every journalist on every music paper, you'll still be left with a substantial amount left that you could sell.

Sell enough and you could recoup all your costs, meaning that your promotional effort has become self-financing. So even if you don't get a deal, at the end of the day you haven't actually *lost* any money.

But how to get them into record shops?

If you've got a bit of a local reputation, then you may be able to sell directly to local record stores. But even if you have the time and energy to drive around the country offering your product to other stores, you're not likely to get many takers if you're pretty much unknown outside your own locality.

That's where distributors come in.

Britain benefits from a very high profile independent distribution network.

Relatively big indie distributors like Rough Trade made their reputations out of taking chances on small unknown bands' products, and are still perfectly approachable today if you're in the unknown one-off bracket.

This is both bad news and good news.

The bad news is that so many people finance their own singles these days that distributors will not be sufficiently impressed by the fact that you're yet another of them to take on your product regardless of what they think about it.

The good news is that if they like you, they may go further than just taking your record – they may help to finance it.

If you're gigging regularly and getting press, a distributor who likes your music and feels it's right for the market may well consider it worthwhile to pay for the costs of pressing your record.

Some distributors will even go as far as paying for the recording! In this respect they're acting like record companies (many of them actually *are* labels as well), but unlike record company deals, you – the artist – retain most of the control.

Costs

If a distributor takes your offering, you can expect a rake-off of between a quarter and a third of the selling price to go to him. However, since you normally supply on a 'sale or return' basis, the distributor takes his cut *only* on records he actually sells into stores.

This is a good system because a) it encourages him to promote your product (no sales – no rake-off) and b) he can't fiddle his cut since any unsold records are returned to you and he must pay you for the rest.

Remember: if a distributor takes your record, the distributor pays you. You do not pay the distributor. Do not do business with anyone who asks for money up front to distribute your records.

Will distributors take cassettes? Some will, some won't.

Will distributors take CDs? Yes.

Will distribution of a self-made record get you a hit? Quite possibly. Modest sales can get you into the indie charts, from which crossover to the mainstream charts is always a distinct possibility. And, as pointed out elsewhere, as little as 500 sales in chart return shops can be enough to get you into the Gallup Top 50. And that's what you want, isn't it?

Books

Music Week Directory edited by David Dalton (Spotlight)

The Making Music Handbook (Track Record)

Big Life, currently the most successful Indie label, made their name in the late '80s dance music craze. 'The Only Way is Up' earned Yazz a gold disc, and helped Big Life to a place in annual singles bestsellers' charts along with the likes of EMI.

THE BIZ

•▶•▶•▶ *Know it – but don't show it*

OPINION differs as to whether a degree of understanding about the business side of the music business helps or not.

Some say that knowledge of what makes 'the biz' tick, how not to get ripped off etc, can only be a good thing. The argument against says that if you understand too much about what goes on behind the scenes, a) you won't have time to play your music, b) you'll get so depressed about it all that you'll just pack it in and c) it just ain't rock 'n' roll.

The last argument is possibly the most powerful. The job of a hit-making musician is to be exciting. Common sense, logic, and reason may tell you that you need to understand accounting and copyright law, but who's interested in a pop star with common sense, logic, and reason?

You can become too aware of the business; spend too much time worrying about points and 'at source' deals and not enough time producing uninhibited, earthy, honest pop music. Truly corporate rock, with everyone a clued-up, info-packed wise guy, is a depressing thought indeed.

So read the following chapter with care: observe, digest, absorb. But just don't let it show!

Managers

'When I first knew Elvis he had a million dollars worth of talent. Now he has a million dollars.' – Col Tom Parker in 1965.

Managers are the most visible, most talked about, and yet least understood people on the business side of things. Everyone knows what an accountant does, what a lawyer does, even what a publicist does (or is supposed to do), but a manager? They manage of course, like producers produce.

The similarity with producers extends further than their shared, rather grey job description. Top managers can get away with huge percentages and watertight contracts because they are top managers. But how did they get there? The chances are they got there through one act.

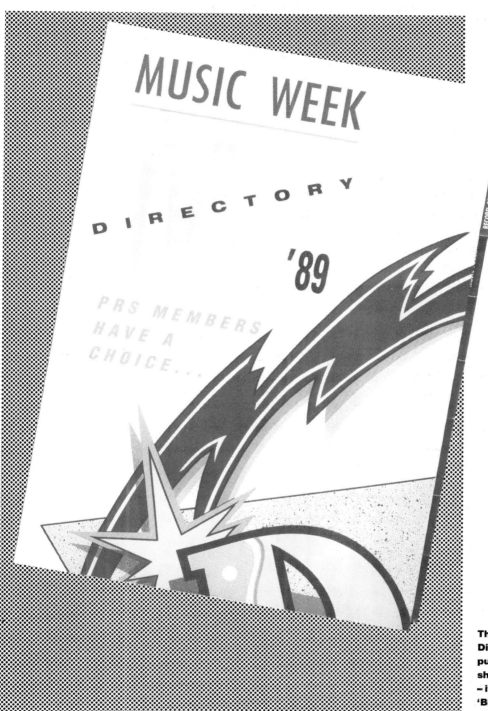

The Music Week Directory, published annually, should be your bible – it contains all the 'Biz' addresses you will need.

Colonel Tom Parker (right) said in 1965 of the man he managed (left): 'When I first knew Elvis he had a million dollars worth of talent. Now he has a million dollars.' And look what he spent it on...

But was that association formed out of brilliant foresight or just luck? Did success come because of the manager, in spite of, or did it make no difference either way?

Unquestionably the right manager can help you gain a hit record. Equally, the wrong one can ensure that you don't – ever. And the most confusing thing is that the right person for you may be the totally wrong choice for someone else. It's all about chemistry, and timing.

What they do and why you need them

Most people starting off think they need a manager to get them a record deal. And they're probably right. Even an okay manager should be able to argue your case more convincingly than you. A manager 'looks better' too.

But a manager's true value comes later – after you've got a deal. It's at this stage that the hard-earned skills of hustling, diplomacy, brinkmanship and favour-extracting come into play. While you're busy writing and recording, a manager should be fighting for a fat promotional budget, tour support, independent pluggers . . . whatever it takes to convert your music into a hit.

You're not likely, actively, to look for such a person, but the Svengali type, who plots and plans your every move, has been notoriously successful. You may *need* such a person; you may, to some extent, benefit from the association; but wholehearted recommendation of the breed is difficult.

Part of the reason the job of manager is so hard to define is that it covers such a wide area; conceivably everything aside from musical decisions on stage or in the studio comes under the managerial brief. As far as the business of making records goes, a manager's job is concerned with extracting as much as possible out of the record company in terms of money and commitment – two things that are neither pre-ordained nor inflexible when it comes to deciding who, out of the company's complete roster of artists, will get the biggest push this month or year.

Success at this particular game is often down to the level at which the lobbying is made. More will be achieved in a single half hour's lunch with the MD than from a month's worth of pub lunches with middle management. The point is, can your manager get to the MD in the first place?

Your manager is the vital link between you and the record company. It may come as a shock to hear that, having signed you, record companies would prefer not to have to see you again except at obligatory do's or for the occasional drink down the pub. But that's the truth. Record companies prefer to deal with one person, and one person who is conversant in music-business business.

How much – How long?
The precise terms are negotiable but the going rate is 20 per cent of the gross income from all music business sources (few will want a share in your paper round, but there again few will want you doing anything else anyway). This means that if you get a publishing advance of £20,000, your manager will automatically relieve you of £4000. You play three nights at Wembley and take home £100,000. Kiss goodbye to £20,000.

Precisely how managers take their cut is up to you. If you entrust the handling of your finances to them, they'll simply pay out 80 per cent of what you would have earned. If, on the other hand, you prefer to look after the money yourself, or hire an accountant, then your manager will invoice you at regular and agreed intervals.

There are many (including managers) who feel this second system is the one less likely to end in tears – artist mistrust of money-handling being the most common cause of management/artist break-ups.

A written management contract is by no means inevitable. Many people trust verbal agreements, the thinking being that if it goes wrong, it's going to GO WRONG and a contract is neither going to cure the problem nor prevent it from happening in the first place.

However most management contracts run from two to three years, with options (unlike those on a record contract) on both sides. Sometimes an established act, changing management, will demand a honeymoon period of six months or so.

The question of management expenses is always difficult. . . . Manager and artist in bar after show one night . . . artist offers manager a drink: accepted and paid for. Manager's round comes up; manager offers artist a drink: accepted and paid for.

Back home . . . when the tour accounts are being presented, artist sees 'Drinks at . . .' on the manager's expense sheet. Unfair? Possibly, but such things happen all the time. If you want to maximise a relationship with your management. thrash out all such problems, likely situations and eventualities right at the beginning. Once trust is broken between artist and manager, the end – and invariably an expensive one all round – is only a matter of time.

Mate or professional management company?

It's not so much that you'll ever be confronted by a straight choice between these two, but some thought on the subject may prevent you making a bad decision when either option presents itself.

To begin with, both types have their advantages, and either can turn into the other, so there are no hard and fast rules.

At the start of a band's career, encountering a friend/a geezer who works in the local club/a sister or brother of the drummer who'll offer their services as manager is probably going to be a monthly occurrence.

You may be tempted to say yeah, okay, and get on with the music but, boringly, don't. Not just like that, anyway. An innocently accepted management agreement can spell big trouble if, just as you're about to sign some major deal, up pops this figure from your past to claim 20 per cent of all your earnings.

But properly organised and legitimised, a manager who was once just a friend or a fan can be the best choice. What he may lack in music business experience, he'll make up for in drive and what can only be described as fire in the eyes. After all, his ascendance up the ladder is directly linked to yours. He will be struggling just as hard to make an impression as a manager as you are as a musician.

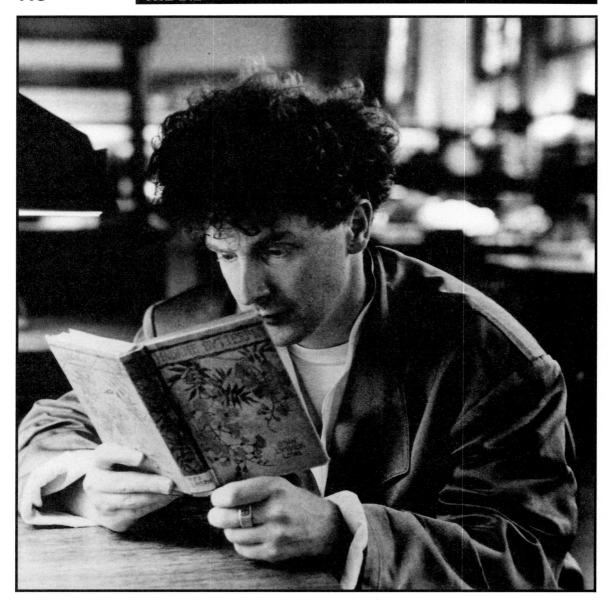

The alternative is a professional management company. The interesting thing about professional management companies is that they're mostly run by people who started out managing on a personal basis.

So what? Well, although such companies may end up with rosters of artists and large, well-appointed offices in the West End, closer inspection may reveal either or both of the following:

First, if the artist on whom the company has grown up is still around, you will always, at best, be number two on the company's list of priorities. Secondly, and

Malcolm McLaren is probably the most famous 'svengali' in the business. You may not want someone like him to plot your every move, but the approach has been notoriously successful.

in no small part due to the first, no 'secondary' artist will ever match the success of the original.

Signing to a large management company does have its compensating factors of course, especially in the area of industry 'clout'. Such companies should be able to pull strings when it comes to acquiring a certain producer, or getting you on the perfect support tour (though be aware that the perfect support tour can be supporting the company's main act – perfect for *them* in other words), and they should be able to exert some leverage with the media, record companies etc by pulling the age-old trick of 'we'll give you access to our main act if you'll also take a look at these guys'.

Such power is not to be underestimated . . .

The manager of a legendary rock band was attending a 20th Anniversary Party being thrown by the band's record company. Throughout the evening various industry figures filed past to congratulate the manager on his success with the band and, at the same time, to find out what else he had on the go. Which was nothing, as it happened.

But somehow the impression got around that the manager had a new act in the wings. Finally the MD stormed up to him. 'How come?' he demanded, 'I've supported you for 20 years now and I'm the only person here who doesn't know about your new act! How much do you want for them?'

After some to-ing and fro-ing, a deal was struck and the chairman wrote a cheque out there and then – for an act that didn't even exist. The manager toyed with the idea of finding an act to fit the advance but finally decided to tear up the cheque and return it.

How do you find a manager?

Management companies are not talent scouts. Unless you're a well-known act already, rarely will they find you. You will have to approach them. On the other hand, individual managers do tend to 'discover' artists themselves.

Nik Kershaw put an ad in the back of *Melody Maker* to the effect of 'I can deliver – get me a deal'. Others have simply contacted management companies direct with tapes and photos, much as if they were approaching a record company.

There are few golden rules with managers except BE VERY CAREFUL. Don't sign anything until you know all the ramifications of the deal including, and especially, everything to do with the finances.

Finally, don't be too greedy or clever for your own good. Management is not an easy job and if done well it deserves the rich rewards. The maxim that 80 per cent of something is better than 100 per cent of nothing is well worth keeping in mind.

● ● ● ● ● ● ● ➤ A list of management companies can be found in the annual *Music Week Directory*.

● ● ● ● ● ● ● ➤ *Expensive Habits* by Simon Garfield (Faber & Faber), a book detailing various music industry court cases, notably management wrangles, should be compulsory reading before signing a management contract.

Nik Kershaw found a manager by putting an ad in the music press to the effect of 'I can deliver – get me a deal'. The manager did get him a deal, and he did deliver . . . for a while, anyway.

Lawyers

Lawyers may not be the most riveting of people and they may talk in a language you only quarter-understand (even that seeming pretty irrelevant), but unless you pay them some attention, you might either miss out on the deal that would have given you a hit, or, miss out on most of the money it generated.

For the first 20 years of rock 'n' roll, the only time musicians went to see lawyers was when they needed to get out of some (normally horrendous) management, recording or publishing deal. By the early '80s, things had improved to the stage where people were at least taking contracts to lawyers *before* they signed them. Nowadays the smart musicians make the lawyer's office their first port of call – before they've even visited a record company or publisher. And some would even recommend you pay a visit as soon as you form the band.

While this should prevent the signing of slavedriving 'you do all the work and I'll take all the money' type contracts, the like of which scores of artists found themselves shackled to in the '60s and '70s, there's also a feeling (among, it has to be said, the very types of people who used to issue them) that this new-found savvy is unmusicianly, 'not rock 'n' roll' and, ultimately, counter-productive. The phrase 'well they would, wouldn't they?' somehow springs to mind.

The fact remains that most of the character traits that make you want to become a pop musician in the first place (like being impulsive, arty, irrational, influenceable . . .) can hardly be described as assets in the world of business and high finance.

Frankly, the sooner you get yourself kitted out with a lawyer the better. And not just any old lawyer. Don't make the mistake of hiring a friend or family relative just because he or she is a solicitor and may be cheap. Because if things ever go wrong, a non-specialist is going to get eaten alive. Go to a recognised music business lawyer, a UK listing of whom you'll find in the *Music Week Directory*.

In the UK, it is most unlikely you'll find a law firm that will take you on for a percentage of the gains (recording advance etc) basis. You'll have to be prepared to stump up anything as much as £150 per hour for the lawyer's time, and for the full handling of a contract negotiation, you're looking at a bill of between £1,000 and £5,000 depending upon how complex and haggled over the negotiations become.

But top firms are more than capable of making approaches to record companies, publishers, or managers on your behalf, and a recommendation from a top firm of music business lawyers speaks volumes.

As mentioned, for bands, there's even a case to be made for seeing a lawyer before you've hardly started working together.

OTT though this might seem, many a band has split up, or caused its record company to cool off drastically before they've had a chance to prove themselves, through internal ructions over financial splits, credits, publicity – things that could have been talked over and settled earlier.

When you start a band you're all equal, you're all broke, you're all unknown. If you're going to make it though you're going to have to deal with realities such as the writers, but probably not the rest of the band, getting publishing monies, the lead singer automatically being assumed to be the spokesman etc. A brief meeting with a lawyer before such eventualities occur can save, at best, unnecessary heartache, and possibly professional suicide, later on.

An early consultation can also be useful for informing or reminding the inexperienced artist about some of the classic do's and don'ts, numbered among which are:

● ● ● ● ● ● ● ◗ Don't ever pay to get your song published
● ● ● ● ● ● ● ◗ Always come to a lawyer before signing anything that smacks of a contract
● ● ● ● ● ● ● ◗ Don't waste time negotiating with a production company

Accountants

Hiring an accountant is not exactly in the red star category before you look set to have a hit record.

However, should you want to maximise your earnings from the same, a specialist music business acccountant will be able to advise you on such things as bank accounts, VAT, tax, how and when to buy equipment, and all manner of dull-sounding topics that, believe it, will spring into life should you fall foul of the financial authorities later on.

An accountant is unlikely to have any direct bearing on whether you make a hit record or not, but helping you to keep some of the money that should accrue is nonetheless pretty worthwhile.

Accountants' charges are normally set per year's worth of accounts. The work they must undertake alters depending upon whether you're an individual, a partnership or a full-blown company. How you structure your business now will effect how much hassle, money, time, you have to spend on the subject later on. Make sure you ask about all the possibilities and at least try, though it ain't easy, to understand the principles.

Agents

An agent's bearing on your hit record (or not) is slim, the job being to procure 'engagements' for you as a performer, be it live, on TV, or even film.

As with publicists, agents have two modes of play: the first being to persuade clubs, tours, whatever, to take you on when you're unknown and nobody is particularly bothered by you, and the second being fending off the offers once you've had record success and are now a sought after commodity.

Though some will try to convince you that it was their skill which propelled you from one camp into the other, in general agents respond to situations but rarely do they create them.

Having said this, hit records can be initiated by sales from a loyal following built up through live work (see page 178), so the choice of agent (even though a baddun isn't as disastrous as a useless manager or record company) needs to be thought out carefully.

As in so many other areas of the music business, it's at the start of your career, when you need the most help, that help is so difficult to find. The fear of making a wrong move – signing, booking, writing about, working for the wrong act – is a universal obsession.

For an agent to say 'yes, okay, we'll give you a try' carries no real risk since he'll not, aside from telephone calls and faxes, be putting any money into you. In this respect, time and energy finding an agent can prove worthwhile, since you will be seen in a better light by subsequent businessmen – managers, record companies, publishers – if someone else has already made some form of commitment.

But nobody ever wants to be the first person to say 'yes.'

You can approach an agent any number of ways, the tape-through-the-post method being by far the most common and the least effective; less effective even than the same routine for record companies, since agents are not worried about how you sound in a studio, but what you sound and look like *live*.

Personal recommendation or just plain badgering is best, and although a proper agency agreement can extend for many years (normally five), most will, after a while, give you a break and see if you can cut the mustard on one or two bookings.

Agents' fees are worked on straight percentages: 15 per cent of the gross being the norm with, sometimes, a reduced rate of say 10 per cent should the engagement pay more than a specified sum. How monies flow is negotiable. Agents will either invoice you for their fee or collect all monies and account to you at agreed intervals, minus their cut.

Don't expect too much in the way of guidance and free advice from agents. Although they'll want you to succeed, of course, they are not in the business of helping you with your image, choice of material etc.

Publicists

Some would argue that, on the totem pole of music business personnel, the publicist lies at the bottom of the heap. Similar to (though worse than) agents, publicists can (and therefore do) do very little for an unknown artist, and for the megastar, they simply weed out the plum interviews/appearances from the pile of requests.

What they will do, though, is happily charge unknowns a fat weekly fee for getting exposure on the strength of the fact that they 'handle' Paul McCartney or Michael Jackson – you know, people for whom it must be really difficult getting media attention.

In other words, if you do all the work for them, ie have 18 number one hits, murder someone, marry into royalty or are a natural media hound, they'll beaver away like crazy getting you all the publicity you (now probably don't) want.

If, on the other hand, you're a regular bunch of guys in a band that's just releasing its first single and have no remarkable features other than (let's hope) musical ability, forget it.

The most you can hope for out of your £250-plus a week fee would be a few clippings of record reviews (which would have been done anyway), and maybe an interview in an instrument mag.

In terms of gaining a hit record, the value of media exposure is immeasurable. The question is, do publicists really help turn unknowns into household names? And the answer is: extremely rarely. Be warned.

Pluggers

You may never encounter a real live plugger and yet go on to produce massive hit after massive hit. The reasons for this could be twofold: you make classic, brilliant records that radio stations are just bursting to play without any prompting, or your record company has a very efficient team of in-house pluggers on the payroll.

In other words, knowing who pluggers are and what they do is not essential if you want to make hit records. All the same ... pluggers can be hired independently of the record company's own team, and vital such a move can be.

In an ideal world you make a record, it's good, DJs and producers of radio programmes hear it (because they spend large chunks of each day listening to all the new releases), they play it to death, it's a hit.

In the real world however, DJs and radio stations don't have time to 'discover' all the best records for themselves – they need a little help or persuasion in the shape of someone shoving your record (at the very least) under their nose over a large G&T in the BBC Club every afternoon for a week.

Of course pluggers don't only work on the Beeb – they also deal with local radio and pirate radio, along with the most influential dance clubs. Who they plug to, for how long, and how successful your record becomes in their hands, are all factors that determine how much you'll have to pay. £1,000 worth of plugging probably won't get you very far, but it'll get you started.

How to choose the best plugger for your record is another matter. There aren't too many to choose from at any given time, and word of mouth is always the best bet. The deal you (or your representatives) strike is important, and a sliding scale 'incentive' arrangement whereby a higher chart placing earns more money is probably the most effective guarantee of effort. When you've got your hit, you're unlikely to worry about the £3,000–5,000 plugger's bill. A list of pluggers can be found in the annual *Music Week Directory*.

Useful 'business' organisations include:

The Society of International Songwriters & Composers – an independent help organisation supplying info on a whole range of songwritery topics. Small membership fee. 12 Trewartha Road, Praa Sands, Penzance, Cornwall TR20 9ST (0736-762826).

Performing Rights Society – collection agency for performance royalties. You only can join once you've had a few record releases so don't worry about it until then. 29–33 Berners Street, London SW7 2AS (01-580-5544).

Musician's Union – which you'll need to join in order to use most session players, and to appear on TV. 60–62 Clapham Road, London SW9 OJJ (01-582-5566).

Central Entertainment Agents Council – organisation supplying info on agents and generally overseeing fair play. 64 Port Street, Evesham, Worcs WR11 6AP (0386-442819).

British Academy of Songwriters, Composers, and Authors – practical help through seminars and newsletters from the experts. Small subscription. 34 Hanway Street, London W1P 9DE (01-436-2261).

Books

Music Week Directory edited by David Dalton (Spotlight)
Making Music Handbook (Track Record)
The Town & Country Club Music Guide, Anna Jenkins & Oliver Smith (T&C)
Breakin' Into the Music Business, Alan Siegel
Expensive Habits, Simon Garfield (Faber & Faber)
Tax & Financial Planning, Richard Baldwin (Butterworths)

User's Guide To Copyright (Butterworths)
Getting Noticed – A Musician's Guide To Publicity & Self-Promotion, James Gibson (Omnibus)
Making Money Making Music (No Matter Where You Live), James W Dearing (Omnibus)
Making It In The New Music Business, James Riordan (Omnibus)

RECORD
COMPANIES

●▶●▶●▶ *Corporate giant or tiny indie, it's the people who count*

ALTHOUGH it is possible to record, press, and distribute your own record, run your own label, publish your own songs, manage yourself ... the vast majority of hits have gone through the standard record company machine: an act has been discovered, signed up, put in a studio, groomed by the marketing men, and finally unleashed onto the waiting public.

Styles come and go, companies come and go, even the recording media come and go (from vinyl to tape to CD to DAT to ?) but the system remains the same. And it remains eagerly sought after. What young musicians have *not* spent half their adolescence fantasising about signing a record deal?

How, followed by who, are the two most difficult nuts to crack. The how part will take some time but we can dispense with the who part fairly swiftly: there's no such thing as a perfect record company, a company that everyone loves, about whom no one has a bad word to say. The reason is that record companies are only as efficient or likeable as the people who work in them, and the people who work in them tend to swop from one company to another with almost indecent haste.

True, some companies are larger than others and some specialise in a particular type of band or style of music. But it's the *people* who count; the people who sign you and the people who'll be looking after you once you've signed.

The problem with record companies is that it's not the *people* you sign to. You sign to the company.

The classic bum deal is when a band has been eagerly pursued by one member of an A&R team *only*, is signed, and then that A&R person leaves, leaving the band signed to a company in which there's not one member of staff really rooting for them.

There's no special safeguard against this, except trying to make sure your appeal is broad based within the company you're talking to, before you sign. In theory, this is always the case; most companies will tell you that no artist gets signed without the full ratification and agreement of the rest of the team and the MD etc. But that's in theory.

Getting
signed up

There are several myths surrounding the signing of record contracts, the most seriously misleading being that they somehow represent the pot of gold at the end of the rainbow, the end of the struggle, the Holy Grail.

The signing of a record contract signifies, if anything, the end of the beginning, your first foot on the ladder. By no means is it an automatic passport to a hit record.

Advice on how to get signed up is now so prolific that any young hopeful not aware that you should always send in tapes addressed to a particular person, send in no more than three tracks – your best first – and a pic etc would have to have spent the past decade on a croft in the Hebrides or something.

Sad to say, much of this advice is wishful thinking. Sending in a tape – addressed personally or otherwise – is an almost complete waste of time. The number of acts signed from such a gambit is infinitesimal. You're better off doing the pools and waiting until you can finance a record on your own.

That's not to say you should forego demos and photo sessions – both are well worthwhile. Rather, you need to work out a game plan that's a little more advanced than packing up the demo and photo and sending it off, unexpected, to a dozen record companies.

To understand why this is so, you need to understand about who works for A&R (Artists & Repetoire) departments, and how they operate.

At the head of the department is the Head of A&R. He/she may or may venture out at night combing the clubs for new talent, but the chances are against it. The chances are, however, that this person is the 'name' you will have found to send your tape to. The chances are 100 per cent that this person's secretary, when confronted by your tape (along with three million others), will automatically pass it on to one of the minions in the department. In other words your finding out a name will not have helped in the least.

Within a company's A&R department, there are scouts of varying importance, in varying areas of the country, and in varying modes of employment. Within the business as a whole, you'll find packs of these people doing the rounds of the clubs, pubs, universities, all LOOKING FOR YOU.

They are what's known in some circles as the Sheep Patrol, you being the sheep that these Ghia-driving, bomber-jacketed, under-25-year-old 'wolves' are out on the prowl for. This collection of A&R scouts figures, quite rightly, that it's no use being stuck out in Reading one night if the real action is going down at the Rock Garden. Moreover, as individuals, there's no way they're going to be so lucky as to appear at the right place at the right time every single night. It's called safety in numbers. And what follows, if an act is worth following, is some form of auction. More of which anon.

Needless to say, the skill comes in making sure that, when the time is right, the Sheep Patrol's venue for the night is *your gig*.

The point of this whole saga is that, although you may think it's you on the lookout for a record company, what the record companies want to think is that *they found you*. Kudos, cred, and money will be heaped upon the A&R scout who 'found' what turns out to be a successful act. If the act becomes really successful, in fact, a person's whole future in the business will be based on the fact that 'he found so and so'.

There's no way the mileage to be gained out of such discoveries is going to be relinquished through stories of a band discovering themselves as it were. The quickest route to a deal is to understand the game and to play along with it for all you're worth.

That's the some-will-say cynical, business aspect of getting a deal; something that your manager should know (and if he doesn't you should worry about whether you've found the right person for the job). Music and your own personality also come into play.

Ask a hundred A&R men (and almost universally they are men) what they're looking for in a new act and they'll mention words like original, fresh, different, unique. The answer to that has to be the question: 'Well why are the charts so full of people who all sound the same? *Someone* must have signed them.'

Yes, in theory, record companies are looking for the Next Big Thing – Punk, New Age, Hip Hop – and would love to have signed the outfit that spawned it. But pragmatism, reality, money, greed, call it what you will, will win out in the end and what most companies are actually looking for is their own version of another company's successful act. And so it goes on.

However, record companies are not completely dumb and predictable. They can also, like the public, spot a phoney. It's no use looking at a successful act and figuring you can 'do that' if, deep down, you wouldn't be comfortable in that style or wearing those clothes. Cloning's fine. But it can't be forced.

Nor can originality. You either incline towards looking like or sounding like you do *naturally*, or it'll come across not so much original as just plain idiotic.

Then there's the question of personality, or attitude – something touched upon in the *Image* chapter. For you to be offered a deal, a record company must think you're serious about the music business. Preferably, moreover, that you're an 'artist' with, if that's how it goes, a typically 'artistic' temperament. This can translate into being simply arrogant, it can be downright stroppy or, in extreme cases, unapproachably rude and/or violent. What record companies don't want to see (or if they claim they do, are ultimately bored by) is a bunch of sane, reasonable blokes who do what they say they're going to do by the time, and for the money, they said they were going to do it.

Your natural feelings may be to 'see the other person's point of view' or to 'be nice and polite', but such an attitude will do your cause no good whatsoever. They'll walk all over you. To get respect, you need to do things like stroll into a record company executive's office as if you own the joint, insist that the company double its last offer and then trash the place.

You'll have noticed that so far in this chapter, advice has been more on a philosophical than a day-to-day 'send your tape in a pink envelope' type of level. But there are no magic action and effect recipes here. For every deal that's signed there'll be a different story: met in pub; mugged A&R guy then handed him a tape; manager blackmailed Sheep Patrol into turning up at gig; MD fancies the drummer; heard last year's indie single. . . .

Clinching the deal

Once you have generated record company interest – in other words they start calling and leaving messages for you – there's no excuse for letting them off the hook.

If the way you were first spotted was playing live, now is the time that those demos and photo sessions will come into their own. If you were introduced by tape, you'll maybe have to start thinking about showcase gigs (see page 182).

Either way, the quickest route to a signature is to let the interested company know that they are not alone in looking at you. Ideally, of course, they won't be alone. You may hear that this is the quickest way to be told to go and take a hike. Who told you that? Someone who works for a record company, probably, and don't believe a word of it.

However, in this instance, deliberate bloody-mindedness, like snagging studio time from one company and playing the tape to another company first, is a double-edged sword: the company might love your confident cheek. On the other hand, they might just send you the bill.

You probably won't encounter much trouble in hinting at other interested parties because soon enough, the fact that you are an act that someone has deemed worth bothering about will be common knowledge among the Sheep Patrol and its paymasters. Resulting in genuine interest from all corners.

The immediate function of such multilateral interest is to bump up your asking price which, if handled by a true expert, can result in negotiations reaching fever pitch before too long. The more you appear unimpressed by each new structure and figure on the table, the more hungrily you will be pursued. Just a plain old fact of life, this one.

The only danger on the horizon is accepting the wrong deal. The largest financial offer may seem the best choice but that's not always the case.

So when considering any offer, ask yourself:

● ● ● ● ● ● ● ▶ Do you have any empathy with the company?

● ● ● ● ● ● ● ▶ How many people do you know (and appear to like you) there?

● ● ● ● ● ● ● ▶ How much control are you being offered (producers, studios, sleeves etc) and how much do you want?

● ● ● ● ● ● ● ▶ How influential is the company (or its contacts) worldwide?

● ● ● ● ● ● ● ▶ What is its reputation?

● ● ● ● ● ● ● ▶ Can you speak to other artists on the label beforehand?

The deals

The best deal for making hit records is the one you've got. Hits are born out of positive thinking. The contract you sign may not be the largest in history; it may not be the largest on the label that year; it may just be a singles deal. But it's the contract you'll be working under, so once you've accepted the terms, accept them. Until you've had a couple of hits, anyway.

Your lawyer and/or manager will attempt to explain in detail what you're being offered and how, if possible, the terms can be improved upon.

Although no two final contracts are the same, there are three basic types of deal you'll encounter: a singles deal, a full recording contract, and a leasing or lease-tape deal.

Singles deal

As the title implies, this is a relatively short term offer by the record company to make and release a specific number of singles, normally within a specific period of time. The advances you'll be offered may not sound magnificent, nor may the implied commitment. But it cuts both ways. If the record company isn't strapping you to its bosom for eternity, then should things not work out between you, you're more likely to be able to salvage your career and move on elsewhere.

Conversely, if you do get a single away under this arrangement, you'll be in a very strong position to negotiate a full recording contract. A singles deal can be an excellent trial marriage for both parties.

Full recording contract

If a record company believes you to have not only some hit material for today's market but also potential for long-term development, then a recording contract that ties you to them for a number of years (normally five, sometimes three) is what you'll be offered.

The small print in your contract has no bearing on whether you make hit records or not. It just governs whether or not you make any money out of them.

It has become popular to think, however, that the more you can sting your record company for in advances, the harder they'll work for you in order to get their money back. Although this has a certain ring of truth to it, logic and common sense are not high on most record companies' list of attributes.

Commitment, in terms of money, people, tour support, videos etc, is the thing to insist upon. Money paid to you in advances is, literally, advance payment for all the records you're going to sell.

Okay, so you won't have to pay it back if they don't sell, but better by far to go for contractual clauses that increase the chances of your *earning* vast sums of money, instead of those that just *advance* you the stuff.

The fine print – whether various expenses in addition to basic recording costs are recoupable, ie whether, ultimately, it's the record company or you that foots the bill – are things to discuss with your manager and lawyer. It hardly needs to be said that you want as much as possible to be non-recoupable – i.e. *they pay*.

Leasing deals

Under this large and rather shambling umbrella come all manner of arrangements, from a low budget DIY record company getting distribution through one of the majors to being conned by some shyster 'producer' into signing with his production company.

In other words be careful.

The basic principle of leasing deals is that you are offering, instead of your raw and unrecorded talent, finished master tapes primed and ready for release.

How the recording came to be made is the question. You may have found a private benefactor with whom you have a straightforward financial arrangement, it could be 'free' studio time from a studio (in return for percentage points), or a club, your parents or your bank might put up the money.

In theory, such deals are attractive because you retain not only so much control over your output, but also – again in theory – so much more of the money, should the records become hits. How much of this is true depends on with whom you strike the deals and how interested you are in playing record companies. Unless you go in with your eyes WIDE open, most leasing deals will end up sapping you of all your energy – musical or business.

Recording contracts: points to note

● ● ● ● ● ● ● ➤ Options to terminate the contract (annually) will be available only to the record company – not to you.

● ● ● ● ● ● ● ➤ You'll be paid only on 90 per cent of sales – a figure arrived at years ago to compensate for breakages.

● ● ● ● ● ● ● ➤ Advances are paid over a period of time; the 'telephone numbers' you read about are generally totalled up figures representing many years worth of advances, before commissions are taken, before recording costs . . . for the benefit of the media.

● ● ● ● ● ● ● ➤ Watch out for cross-collateralisation: if you're also signing to a company's publishing division or related enterprise, you may find that although you're in credit with one division, you're still in the red with another. Cross-collateralisation means that they can then offset one against the other and so avoid having to pay you yet. If spotted, remove from contract.

● ● ● ● ● ● ● ➤ There's not an artist in history who hasn't either been or felt ripped off. Be prepared to join the club.

Record company staff

Knowledge of who works for record companies and what makes them tick is a vital ingredient in the hitmaking process.

A&R (artistes & repertoire)

The A&R (fondly known as 'Um and Ah') department will be most people's first port of call in the record company. These are the guys that signed you, so you probably know them already. Someone – often but not always the actual person who's claimed responsibility for signing you – will be appointed as your own personal record company contact. It is this person to whom you complain when things are going badly and congratulate when the going gets good.

The Repertoire part of A&R means songs. In theory the department will help you select material, and suggest third party songs whenever necessary or applicable. In practice they'll be out looking for new bands to sign.

The A&R department as a whole will be staffed by people you can probably relate to, a large proportion being made up of ex-musicians. It can also mean they're less likely to be fooled by musicians' foibles, tricks, and guises – yeah, we really do need to hire six different types of keyboard amp!

Although a recording budget will have been thrashed out beforehand, the department can, and frequently has to, sanction additional costs or extensions in time.

You'll need a relationship that allows you to extract what you need from the company without extracting the piss. A bit of wild 'artistic' behaviour never goes amiss but if you totally screw up, the next person out the door behind yourselves will be your A&R contact. Be reasonably reasonable.

One problem that invariably rears its head is whether or not to involve your A&R contact when you're recording. If so, how much, and at what stage? Once the producer and studio have been chosen, demos made and pored over, theoretically, control over your music passes from record company to producer. Some A&R people won't let go; some do but shouldn't have. Though this is something that must be judged, ultimately, on individual merits, the principle of 'too many cooks' tends to apply.

In addition to spoiling the broth, over-involvement can lead to disappointment (the favourite-bit-on-an-early-version-being-left-out-on-the-final-mix-syndrome), which in turn can lead to disillusionment – dangerous states of mind, both.

But a too strictly administered policy of 'mind your own business' can stem a flow of the very enthusiasm you'll need every drop of once your record is made.

Ideally, you need to let the record company *think* they're involved more than, perhaps, they are. If your contact wants to think it was his suggestion you use congas, or push up a particular riff – fine, let him think that.

As already mentioned, your A&R contact's standing within the industry is closely linked with yours (and others he deals with). Although he may work for the record company he is as close to being on your side as it gets. The moral of the story is that if the relationship with your A&R contact is a good one, you'll get the most out of your record company. It should also be said that the reverse – a breakdown being able to spell the end of your career there – is equally true.

Sales and marketing

Depending upon the type and size of company, a whole range of departments and people come under marketing (press, promotions, people called product managers) and sales banners.

Product managers are generally assigned a number of acts to look after; if you like, they're your next 'deeper into the record company' contact within the company, and quite possibly are also ex-musicians.

Their job is to co-ordinate the nuts and bolts of your music from demo to Virgin Megastore; from sleeve design to scheduling release dates.

Without having the make or break power of senior A&R people, product managers are a major link in the chain, and their co-operation and respect should be sought, as new acts who find their status sufficiently low to merit a pre-Christmas release date will testify.

There may or may not be an in-house art department, but product managers will have overall responsibility for things like album sleeves (unless you've stipulated otherwise), logos etc. The point about such material is this: an ace album sleeve and logo isn't going to rescue a duff album; they may help sharpen the focus on a borderline one; they'll be the icing on the cake for a classic. End of story.

A press officer's job is to liaise with the press. Inasmuch as some press officers have better relationships with certain newspapers and magazines than others, press officers are important. But the reality is it's the press itself, not the press officer, who can influence your hitmaking potential.

Among other things like procuring interviews or suggesting you employ a PR agent when all else fails, press officers will be in charge of preparing your press releases. Press releases précis your career and provide all sorts of 'interesting' info on you for journalists to crib off. Generally speaking, they are atrociously written and represent a criminal waste of trees. Try to exert some influence on their style and content if you value your credibility.

Richard Branson presents the most human of record company faces, even though in reality his interests have grown beyond the music industry.

The Promotions department is one off the really sharp end of selling records (sales), and involves itself in getting your records played on radio, in clubs, placing adverts, and at least shooting for TV appearances.

At the end of the day, promotions and sales people are the record company's real heroes, as it is by their efforts that records go into the stores in the first place in order to come out of them under the public's arm. All kinds of bonus schemes and incentives operate in these spheres, and since they very rarely do get to meet the people behind 'the product', occasional 'geeing up' visits to sales force meetings can work wonders. Another one to file under 'plain common sense' really.

Crawling, and/or displays of knowledge about the business are neither necessary nor welcome. Just a good old honest 'Cheers mate' and general chit chat will do nicely.

The MD and the secretaries

You may meet your MD only once (upon signing), twice (upon being terminated), or frequently (whenever your latest release turns gold and you're invited in for a swift glass of bubbly). If your manager is on lunching terms with the MD, this will be of considerable help. The chances are the MD will not want to soil his or her hands with you too often. Probably better that way.

Secretaries, by contrast, are the people you'll spend more time with than anyone else, as you wait for meetings to end or begin, wait to pick up white labels or proof sheets, or hang around waiting for the journalist from *Sounds* to turn up.

Fall foul of the secretaries and it's Goodnight Vienna. Their enthusiasm, opinion at 'consumer level' in the eyes of their boss, and power to make things happen (including cheques being signed) can be critical. Overt sucking up will be spotted in seconds; just be yourself and don't treat them as if they didn't matter. Sexist it may be, but if you're male and in the heartthrob class, an extra sock down the strides during visiting hours won't hurt your chances either. For female artistes, giving the impression of being powerful but not bitchy 'in real life' will go down best.

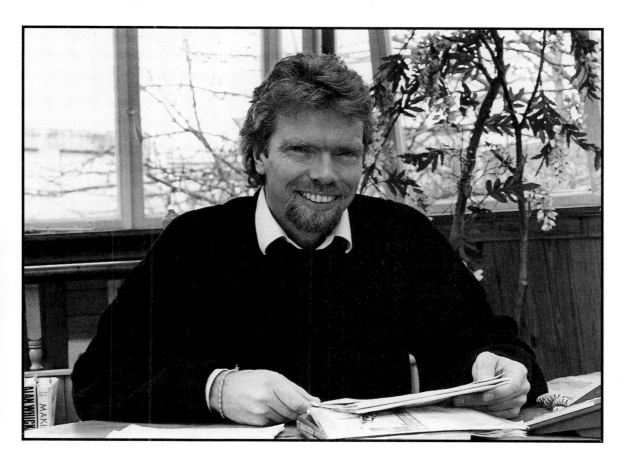

PUBLISHING

●▶●▶●▶ *A licence to print money*

THERE are many ways in which publishers can help you have a hit record: if you're not a songwriter, they can find you a song; if you're only a songwriter, they can place it for you; and if you're both, they can offer you a publishing deal and nurture you along until a record company is sufficiently convinced to offer you a recording contract.

To a small degree, publishers have always done this, but their original and prime purpose was to publish sheet music – something they still do of course, but at a fraction of the level they did in the old days.

What do publishers do?

Back in those old days, when the business of songwriting far outweighed the business of making records, or radio and TV performances (for the simple reason that such media either didn't exist or were in their infancy), publishers had plenty to do: organise the transcription of songs and their printing, organise the selling of songs through live performances to other artists. . . . Accordingly, the rewards for owning copyright of a song were stacked very much in the publishers' favour.

With the decline in sheet music sales, ironically, at the expense of records, radio and TV, two things happened: publishers had less, physically, to do, but they got more money.

Increasingly their role became one of collection and accounting agency for monies automatically set aside for 'publishing', both from the sale of mechanical replay items like records and from the performance of songs live, or on radio and TV. Simply by being the publishers of hits, these companies could sit back and watch the money roll in. They didn't have to demo the song, record it, print it, pay the writer to live . . . nothing.

Things reached absurd levels during the '70s, by which time publishers had reduced themselves to parasites, feeding on the naivity and talents of young songwriters and giving the business almost nothing in return.

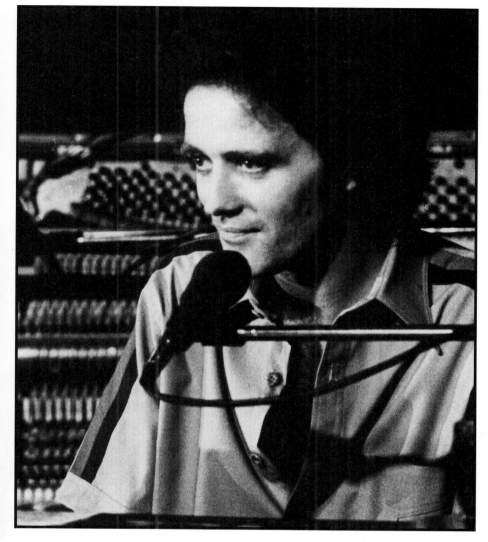

Music publishing has changed radically in the artist's favour since the celebrated '70s court victories of Gilbert O'Sullivan (here) and Tony Macauley against their respective publishers.

A lot has changed, thanks mainly to two highly successful figures of the '70s – songwriter Tony Macaulay and popster Gilbert O' Sullivan – whose separate, celebrated, and successful court cases against their masters have resulted in publishers a) not being allowed to get away with patently unfair or one-sided contracts, and b) writers in general wising up a bit.

Fortunately, publishers have not just 'learnt their lesson', now coughing up decent advances and royalty splits, but they have also re-appraised their role in the music business. Nowadays they can (and do) act as talent scouts, as go-betweens with a record company, as production companies; in other words the days of 'active publishing' appear to have made a comeback.

The full spectrum of publishing extends further than the brief of this book, but

Write a 'B' side and succeed? Funny but true – if your piece is the 'B' side of a hit you get half the royalties.

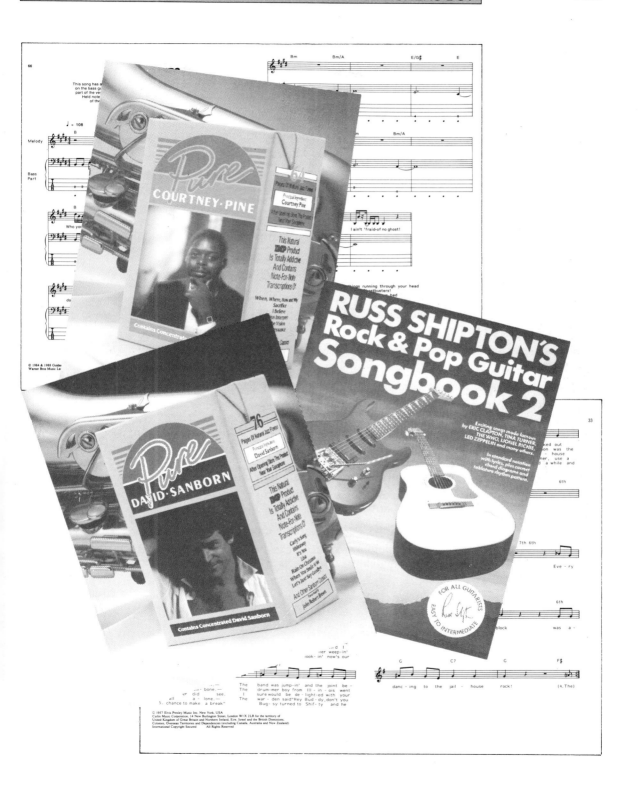

publishing is important because it represents control over your career. And there's money in it.

On a hit record, by the time you've added up mechanical royalties from record sales, the performance royalties from radio, TV, and video, and any sheet music royalties, you're talking bucks!

Accordingly it is a fiercely complex and hard-fought world, and signing over your copyright to a publisher should not be done without careful thought as to who that publisher is, how much you trust the company, and how well you understand the contract that's being offered. Never sign anything without having had the ramifications of it explained in full by your lawyer and manager. But first:

What am I doing by signing a publishing contract?

You're saying to a company: 'You look after my interests for this song, or X number of songs, for Y number of years; you make sure no one rips us off, artistically or financially; if you think we can make money out of it, you organise the printing of some sheet music; you try to persuade other artists to record the song(s). In return I'll split all the money that the material generates within the terms of our agreement.'

In return you may also expect an advance on said money, as in a record contract. An advance might be a one-off paymemt or it might become payable every time an option to renew your publishing agreement is picked up. Either way you won't receive any additional money (each period) until your royalty earnings put you back in the black.

So, you're selling the copyright to a negotiable number of songs for a negotiable period of time (most commonly set at 50 years after your death!) and a negotiable amount of money.

Who gets what and how?

In publishing terms as a whole, earnings from what they call 'mechanical' means, ie from records, tapes etc sold, are calculated at $6\frac{1}{4}$ per cent of their wholesale price plus an additional (and varying) percentage to take the figure up to a notional (since one rarely exists nowadays) list price.

This sum of money is automatically set aside from such sales, and passed along to whoever should receive it by the record company.

Money is also generated by radio, TV, video, and live performance renderings of your songs. A complex but nonetheless legally enforcible system has evolved whereby the 'power' of each medium dictates how much that medium must pay to the copyright holders of each song it uses. You'll get pounds from a play on prime-time national TV; pennies from a play on Radio Mull.

These are the two biggies in terms of where publishing money comes from, channelled through collection agencies – MCPS for mechanicals, and PRS (in the UK) for performance royalties. Where it goes depends upon your publishing agreement. Legally you cannot be fobbed off with less than a 50–50 split.

In practice you'd be nuts to sign such a deal today; 75–25 is perfectly normal and higher splits (in the songwriter's favour!) seem to emerge each year.

PRS

The Performing Rights Society (PRS) is not a body set up to see you're performing right as one BBC jock – was it DLT? – used to wag. Rather it 'collects' money on behalf of songwriters and publishers from radio and TV airplay, and from the loosely apportioned 'performance' of your and other songwriters' material via juke boxes, piped music and radios in stores, the premises where such activity takes place being required to hold (ie buy) a fixed rate annual PRS licence.

It collects money from all round the world; agencies in various foreign territories do their own domestic collections and then, for a fee, pass the money along to PRS. The best known foreign agencies are the American BMI and ASCAP.

You can join PRS only once you've had a couple of songs recorded. There's no fee, but they charge a small percentage of the take.

MCPS

The Mechanical Copyright Protection Society (MCPS) is an organisation that exists to collect monies due from record sales. Theoretically, you don't need to join MCPS to receive your due (based on whatever split has been agreed with your publisher). Your record company can pass it along. Your publisher can pass it along. Or you can join MCPS and get them to pass it along – minus a small (5 per cent) fee. Well, who do you trust?

Advantages of signing a publishing deal before a record deal

● In some cases it may simply be easier. A publisher will not (necessarily) have to commit the same level of money to you as will a record company and so may be more willing to give you a try. The school of thought that says this will make the procuring of a record contract a lot easier has some credibility, as the only way the publisher is going to make money out of you is by *someone* recording your songs – successfully so, too. So you should be able to count on the publisher's assistance. (For the reverse argument see below).

● If the publisher is conscientious, you should be able to develop your songwriting abilities without the pressure of an upcoming album to record. Most publishers will assist some way in providing money or facilities for demos.

● Publishing advances should give you a financial breather so you won't have the pressure to sign the first half-way decent record contract you see - or starve!

● They may then take you more seriously as a *songwriter* and push for 'covers' rather than rely upon your own recordings, which is what generally happens when a publishing deal is signed at or around the same time as a record deal.

Disadvantages of signing a publishing deal before a record deal

● The other side of argument number one above is that having 'signed away' your publishing, you will be a less tempting prospect for record companies with publishing divisions. All will deny this of course, but such factors, though unlikely, frankly, today, may just tip the balance out of your favour.

● Money. This is the most serious reason not to pre-sign publishing. When you're unknown and unproven, the quality of your publishing deal rests on you or your manager's ability to sell conjecture. If you wait until you have a record deal, or, ideally, a hit, then your success will do the talking. If you can afford to do so, and are confident of getting a record deal, holding onto your publishing is the only way to go. You will still collect 'publishing' monies if and when due to you.

Publishing contracts – points to note

- Never pay to have your song 'published'. Absolutely never.
- Insist on an 'at source' deal if signing to a large publisher. This means your percentages are based upon the initial income from a song, not the income your publisher may have received after various associate companies abroad have taken their whack.
- If signing to a sister company of your record/production company, avoid clauses that allow cross-collateralisation.
- Remember that publishers don't really have to 'do' anything any more. So either insert clauses that insist they do (pay for demos, have to get covers or lose rights to the song . . .), or else strike the very hardest split possible and relax about it. Don't feel sorry for them. There's no such beast as a poor publisher.

IMAGE

●▶●▶●▶ *A unified audio-visual package for the public*

FROM '50s drainpipes and quiffs, through psychedelia, flower power, flares, glam rock, punk, and new romanticism, to today's clean cut, boy next door, teeth 'n' smiles look, image has played an important part in music business success.

Would Gary Glitter have taken the '70s by storm in jeans and T-shirt? In their own time, would Boy George, Adam Ant, or Kiss? How would you rate a metal band's chances of success sporting anything other than spray-on Spandex, flowing curly locks and a quivering-tongued grimace?

Even seemingly un-image-conscious artists like Tanita Tikaram or Joan Armatrading present an image to their public; indeed one which they'd be most ill-advised to alter (imagine the reaction from Joan Armatrading fans should the lady change her name to Joanie and come out dressed like Sabrina).

Image is not simply wearing a daft haircut or street *haut couture*; it's more subtle than that. Image is about providing the public with visuals that are compatible with your music, a unified package with which they can identify.

Invariably, image is only a problem to an artist or band that appears not to have one. It's a problem because the best images are natural, in other words a look that the person or group like *anyway*, as opposed to a look they've been forced to adopt.

Should that look be wearing flower pots on their heads – as worn, jauntily, in the early days by the naturally bizarre Devo – or wearing country boy denim – as worn by 'natural country boy' John Cougar Mellancamp – it really doesn't matter. All that matters is that you don't look embarassed by it and that it fits your music.

As mentioned, this is all very well if you're a natural fashion hound, ravishingly good looking and eight feet tall or something. But what to do if you're just a bunch of guys or girls?

You need to do *something* in this age of CDV and MTV, as without an image, at best, your record company or management will always have a stick to beat you with when the hits don't pour in. And, at worst, the hits simply *won't* pour in.

It's often said that you shouldn't go for an image you're not prepared to stroll

Left: Boy George was one of the artists who successfully exploited the early '80s obsession with constantly changing image; he changed his as often as most folk change their underwear.

down to the pub in. True to an extent, though I doubt Gazza Glitter hotfooted it down to the Dog and Fox dressed in all his schmutter too often in his heyday.

Inspiration?

Inspiration for an image can come from almost anywhere: comic books, films, sci-fi . . . or perhaps from somewhere closer to home like a local art or fashion college.

Looking at what other bands are wearing can be dangerous. Okay, so a million bands wear classic things like leather jackets and leather trousers. But if you are seen copying someone else's clearly distinct image, be prepared to be thought a clone.

Looking at related industries – fashion being the most obvious – is another matter. Look, learn, and adapt.

Or perhaps you'll want to retain the services of a 'designer'. Things can be worked out fairly simply, since most designers will, if they have any business sense, use you as way of publicising their wares as much as you are using theirs to publicise yourself.

One final thought is that once you have, knowingly or naturally, got yourself an image, and been successful with it, changing it is going to be tough. But that's another book.

Devo: a naturally bizarre band who satirised pop's obsession with image. The more bizarre their dress – anything from body bags to flowerpot hats – the more seriously they were taken.

Photography

Photographs, right from the first pix you send prospective record companies, help create and promote your overall image, and help fix you in their minds. There may be nothing wrong with a bog standard mug shot, but a well-taken, interesting photograph of an interesting looking band might just stick in the A & R guy's mind long enough for him to feel it's worth donating you a couple of days studio time.

The same 'make them take a second look' rule applies to the news editor of a pop magazine, a DJ, or a television researcher, all of whose cooperation will greatly enhance your chances of having a hit record.

As for who, what, and how, that's your decision, but a photographer who feels privileged to work with you – a student, young professional, enthusiastic amateur, friend – will probably spend more time and care on your photographs

The Wedding Present, a successful self-releasing band whose DIY approach extends to their boy-next-door image.

than the case-hardened pro music biz snapper to who you're just another band. Again, go to art and design colleges, colleges of printing etc. You'll be surprised at how many gifted young photographers will be willing to learn and develop (!) with you.

Taking photographs outside – on a windswept moorland, beside a derelict Gothic church, on the coast – can do wonders; either adding to your image or disguising, somehow, your imagelessness. Whenever you see a neat-looking location, jot it down in a notebook. From such jottings not only an album cover might come one day but songs, or lyrics as well.

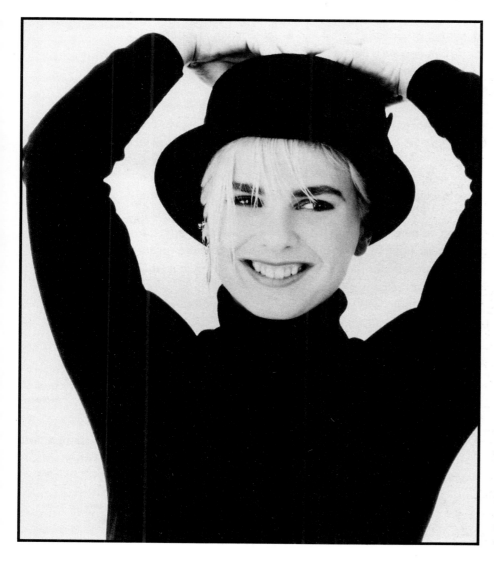

Sam Browne's image comes from the way she sounds rather than the way she looks – a serious singer who happens to be glamorous.

Video

Whether or not a first rate video can turn a second rate record into a hit is debatable, but video is now an accepted, if not insisted-upon, medium in the hitmaking process.

As the cost of the hardware (camera etc) falls, so video as a selling agent becomes more widely expected further and further down the ladder. Not long ago videos were only made for hit artists. Then one became expected with every record release, then for demos, now, sometimes, even to get a booking at a club.

Unless you are a natural visual artist – a budding Bowie or Michael Jackson - there's little point in recommending you spend hours studying video techniques and such. But a contact in the video field never goes amiss: experience at performing to camera, seeing which ideas work and which don't, and a general awareness of the medium can only be a bonus.

If you don't have a friend with a video camera, there are video clubs and courses in most localities.

Once you're in the position of having a record company or management company financing a video to accompany a record release, your control over the situation will probably be similar to that you have over choosing studios and producers.

Many of the same rules apply, the most important of which is: don't get talked into a name director for the wrong reasons. Video directors shoot bread and butter videos too.

Name directors will also come primed with jobs for their particular boys, ie three cameramen, art directors, lighting and sound guys, and sundry jobsworths and hangers on. For all this, you can *certainly* read expensive, but only *possibly* of any value – commercially or artistically.

Young directors, by virtue of their lack of experience, tend to be fuller of and fresher with ideas. Moreover, the public tends to react against obvious displays of expense, unless accompanied by virtuoso artistry (Peter Gabriel's 'Sledge-hammer' for instance).

●●●●●●●▶ The average 'professional' video, financed by record companies, now costs in the region of £30,000.

●●●●●●●▶ Michael Jackson's 'Thriller' cost more than £500,000.

●●●●●●●▶ A list of specialist music business photographers, plus video companies, distributors, duplicators, and production companies can be found in the *Music Week Directory*, published annually.

During her rise to fame in the '80s, Madonna exploited forbidden images for maximum publicity. By playing on the virgin/whore complex, she proved more successful than Superman in making it fashionable to wear your underwear on the outside!

What message do U2's long coats and even longer faces convey? 'We may be mega-rich stadium rockers but we take our responsibilities to the kids very seriously.'

Anti-image as image – Fairground Attraction's skiffle-influenced music looks backward to the '50s, and their visual image reflects this.

Do you remember
Adam Ant's pirate
look? How many
other Ant images do
you recall? Here
was a band whose
flamboyant
expressionism was
perfect for
exploiting the '80s
video boom.

Attitude

Attitude is an intangible but still instantly recognisable by-product of image. Attitude is your stance, your political and social standpoint, and it's something that is becoming increasingly relevant in today's up-front yet behind-the-scenes society.

If you're gay, or a member of the National Front, or Greenpeace, or an Old Etonian, or an ex-prisoner, there may not be a lot you can do – or want to do – to disguise the fact. Does it matter? Is it in fact useful?

In the same way as national newspapers are not content with your sex and age should you receive their attention – you have to be labelled a 'train driver', a 'housewife' or a 'commuter' – the music-orientated public and press respond to attitude identities.

Bands like Genesis and Dire Straits have now been deemed to represent the

Bob Geldof and Midge Ure: two very different images for the two men who worked together to create Band Aid and Live Aid, and who thus become prime representatives of pop's 'green' sensibility.

There is no refuge from Image. Even being un-image-conscious, like Joan Armatrading, is no escape, because that's an image too – and one which works particularly well for her.

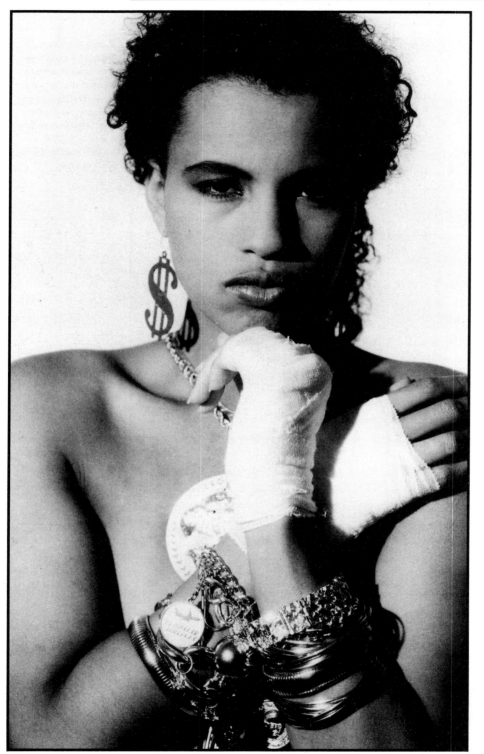

Neneh Cherry is the American dance queen whose first hit, 'Buffalo Stance', exploits the same hook line strategy as Gerry Rafferty's 'Baker Street' (see page 15). Her approach to image is a standard glamorous look – her music is more innovative.

Fine Young Cannibal's exotic visual image is backed with a musicianly approach.

conservative, yuppie, Charles and Di brigade; U2 the rebels without causes; Geldof and Midge Ure the Greens; Sam Fox the tits and arses (literally and figuratively) and so on. . . .

Certain attitudes help a great deal. They'll help cultivate the press (see *Press* chapter, page 164) and they'll help you to build up a following of like-minded people.

But though effective, it can be a dangerous game. First, the attitude you genuinely have may not be the attitude the media think you have and thus project you as having. Secondly, don't try to change courses midstream. Worse than attempting a shift in musical style is an attempted shift in attitude. 'I used to be a money-grabbing, raving chauvinist Tory but now I'm a concerned and liberated Green.' Forget it!

Ten successful rock/pop attitudes

1　Religion (Cliff Richard)

2　Gay (Communards)

3　Sex symbol (Madonna, Tom Jones)

4   Angry young man/woman (Elvis Costello/Patti Smith)

5   Conservationist/humanitarian (Midge Ure, Howard Jones)

6   Tortured 'artist' (Lou Reed)

7   Boy or girl next door/grannies favourite (Bros, Kylie Minogue)

8   Intellectual (Randy Newman, Joni Mitchell)

9   Party animal (Bon Jovi)

10   Mysterious (Michael Jackson, Prince)

THE PRESS

● ◆ ● ◆ ● ◆ *Necessity is the mother of invention*

PUBLICITY has always been a major cog in the hit machine, and it is vital that, as an aspiring hitmaker, you understand how the press works and – more to the point – how it can be made to work for you.

The adage that all publicity is good publicity is one that many of pop's cleverer manipulators live by. Sex Pistols' manager Malcolm McLaren is legendary for demonstrating the rewards of actually engineering what others would regard as 'bad press'. Or, if not having engineered it, at least turning it to instant advantage.

And it's undoubtedly true that many a music business publicist, faced with the need to 'deliver' a minimum number of column inches in the press in return for retainers paid by artists' managements, has found comfort in the old proverb: necessity is the mother of invention.

But a policy of hyping your way, via 'bad' or 'good' press, into the public eye still requires talent – albeit the talent of salesmanship rather than musicianship – and it is foolish to believe that the press will fall for any old rubbish....

No, strike that. It *was* foolish to believe that the press would fall for any old rubbish. But since the popular 'Fleet Street' papers moved in on pop in a big way, the market for trivia, idle gossip, scandal and straightforward, unadulterated lying has really opened up.

Let us suppose for the moment, however, that you're more interested in, at least initially, taking the more traditional editorial route to stardom....

The Music Press

Music papers are always looking for The Next Big Thing. They want to spot it before the record companies (easy), before the daily papers (even easier) and before TV producers (a walkover). They respond to musical talent but also to overall image – do you write good songs, have you got important things to say, do you have a good street level following, do you look good, are you hip, are you *original*?

The music press is your indispensable finger on the pulse – read and digest.

Learn the mysteries of dealing with the music press, and you'll find that you get valuable coverage denied to others. You'll be perceived as interesting, topical, relevant and newsworthy – even if you aren't.

And that can help you substantially in all your dealings with managements, booking agencies, publishers, promoters, record companies, TV, radio, studios and equipment suppliers, as well as raising your standing in the eyes of audiences and record buyers, and of course increasing your chances of getting further press which keeps all the other wheels turning.

The music press has always been faddish, but because of its specialisation, it has the space to give *some* kind of exposure to a very wide range of musical effort, and really *in-depth* coverage to several dozen different artists or bands every week.

This gives it a vital role to play in the exposure of new talent.

Who reads the music papers?

The music press is read mainly by dedicated music fans – committed record-buyers and concert-goers who want more from their reading than to be acquainted with this week's Top Ten and regaled with publicity hype from press hand-outs.

Music press readers want to be *informed*, and expect the writers on their favourite papers to act as a kind of taste filter, helping them, through reviews and other critical articles, to sort out the wheat from the chaff.

Getting into the right papers

Each paper has areas of music it covers extensively, areas it touches on from time to time and other areas it ignores completely. The types of music a music paper covers are part of what give that paper its direction, its image. The way it presents its chosen coverage – the attitudes of the writers, the type of photography, even the style of wording used in headlines – is all part of the paper's personality.

Rule number one, therefore, is: if you want to get press, know your papers.

Be familiar enough with the papers to get a feeling for the differences between them, their particular strengths and weaknesses, their likes and dislikes. Then, rather than just taking haphazard pot shots at getting coverage in your favourite rag, you can actually think of constructing a publicity *campaign*.

Publicists vs self-publicity

Of course, rock publicists exist to do that very job for you, and if you have the funds to employ one, you may be inclined to consider it seriously. After all, you don't have to employ them for life – many publicists will, for just a few hundred pounds, quite happily take a contract to promote, say, a self-financed one-off single over a four week period.

But if you're just starting out, with no track record to speak of, the chances of a publicist being able to get you any column inches you couldn't get on your own are pretty slim. Most will, however, happily go on taking your cash until you realise this.

Publicists, of course, don't just know the papers – they know some of the writers too. And so can you – not necessarily personally, but at least in terms of their tastes. Some papers carry weekly writers' playlists which give you an idea of what they're currently listening to; look for the ones who seem interested in the kind of music *you* make. Read any reviews or interviews covering artists you have been – or think you ought to be – compared to, and note who's written them.

Then, send them a tape, a single and/or an invitation to your next gig and see if you get a reaction.

Make sure that your offering is accompanied at the very least by a contact phone number. Some background information (called a 'biog' in bizspeak) is useful too – but stick to the facts. Don't bother with reams of waffle about your being the best thing since sliced bread because it'll go straight in the bin.

Remember: journalists get dozens of these every week, they've heard it all before and hype of this kind won't impress them.

If you can afford a decent photo session, send a picture too. Black and white glossies are what the papers generally want – not out-of-focus colour prints your mate banged off on the end of a roll of holiday snaps. If you look great in pictures, push the visuals as hard as you can without actually saying please write about us because we look good. If you do, they will, sooner or later.

If you get no reaction within a week, call the writer you sent the stuff to and check whether he/she has received your offering and whether your record/tape has been listened to. If it hasn't, your call will act as a reminder, and your threat to call back in another day or two will usually galvanise the hack into playing your track, just to get you off his/her back.

Dealing with rejection

If your second call gets you a blunt rebuff, there's no point in trying to persuade the writer that he's wrong; accept your rejection gracefully but enquire if your contact thinks there's anyone else on the staff who might be more interested, and follow the procedure as before.

Don't take a polite response as a *sure* sign of interest – it may just be good manners – and don't take friendliness from a writer as a cue to pester the hack night and day in the belief that a double-page spread is just around the corner.

This is most definitely counter-productive, and will get you a reputation as a pain in the arse instead of as an upwardly mobile, talented artist.

Be exclusive to everyone

Spread your PR effort; never pin all your hopes on one writer or one paper. At the same time, however, be aware that 'exclusivity' has a certain attraction within the press, and if you really do have something to offer, then individual writers and papers will often respond well to the notion that you are offering them exclusive access.

This doesn't mean only ever granting interviews to one paper, but it does mean giving different publications different 'scoops' at different times.

And while one particular journalist may not appreciate being the sole target of your every attempt at getting press, it has to be said that the good relationships successful acts have with certain music papers are often due to the efforts of a single writer who supported them in their early struggles.

All the papers naturally hope to reap this kind of benefit; if they spot your budding talent when all around are ignoring you, it seems only fair that you remember them when you make it big.

Building 'em up to knock 'em down?

But ultimately, will they stab you in the back? Is it true, as many musicians who've suffered an unexpected slagging in the pages of a music papers will swear, that the music press only builds you up to knock you down? The answer to that must be a qualified 'no'. Music writers are as much music fans (albeit more privileged ones) as their readers, and like anyone else, they react to the output of their favourite artists.

Anyone with any kind of overview of the music business knows that consistent output (and especially consistently interesting output) is a relatively rare commodity in pop circles and that, in fact, the creative abilities of many artists with supposed long term potential peak at about the third album. So the chances of never getting a slagging are pretty remote. You can but do your best and try to learn from any constructive criticism that comes your way.

And remember this: if a large proportion of pop's would-be megastars *didn't* have a short shelf life, there wouldn't be any room for new talent, ie *you*, to get a look in.

Inside stories

There are many different sections of a music paper in which you might feasibly get some coverage.

NEWS PAGES

These are reserved for information about gigs, tours, label signings, record releases and topical issues which affect the music industry and the consumer. Your gigs, your record releases are news. Send details to the news editor.

GIG GUIDE

Send gig information separately to the editor of the paper's listings or gig guide section. Remember that deadlines for both are at least ten days before the relevant issue hits the streets.

GOSSIP SECTION

These pages are reserved for music business tittle tattle, unverified rumours, outrageous publicity stunts, silly photographs and everything else that doesn't belong anywhere else. In the absence of a scintillating true story, try a little embroidery.

NEWS FEATURES SECTION

Many papers devote several pages to short stories which are a blend of news, gossip and interview material. New talent often features in these sections; find an interesting 'angle' and you have the chance of an 'in'.

REVIEWS SECTION

Essentially for commenting on record releases and live shows, these pages are frequently the first step up the publicity ladder for new acts. A positive review helps you to argue the case for the next level of coverage – a short feature – and will draw attention to you within the business.

TECHNICAL PAGES

Some music papers cover instruments and may run items on musicians and their equipment from time to time. So if you play the only harmonium successfully converted to run on North Sea Gas, tell them about it.

FEATURES PAGES

In the music press, features – usually based around interviews – are the biggest spaces alloted to any one act, and will generally reflect the importance of that act in the eyes of the paper. They may also reflect a lot of other things, for example how much the record company has spent flying journalist and photographer to some exotic corner of the world in order to 'get the story'.

If you're a new act without the backing of a record company PR budget, you'll only get a good-sized first feature if
a) you've established yourself with a very strong single,
b) somebody in your band already has a reputation from previous work,
c) you're getting rave reviews whenever you play live,
d) major labels are chasing you to sign with them, or
e) the editor fancies your singer.

Methods of persuasion

You can buy ads in the music press, but can you buy editorial, which, in terms of influence, is worth around 20 times the same amount of ad space? Does bribery exist in the world of music journalism, and if so, does it work? And what is the effect on journalists of marketing gimmicks such as free tee-shirts or fancily packaged albums?

The most common form of persuasion among record companies is the aforementioned foreign trip. Some papers accept every trip offered while others are more selective, taking only those trips to cover acts that they would have written about anyway.

In the latter case, what the record company stands to gain is a) more space in the paper (because, being in some exotic location, the writer can naturally find more things to write about) and b) a more interesting feature (because the writer can always find something else to write about if the band themselves are desperately dull).

It's also fair to say that this kind of hospitality does tend to reduce the space devoted to possible negative comment, but that said, every record company press officer has stories of expensive trips that have resulted in unmitigated slag-offs. You can't win 'em all – but you can win most of 'em.

When you're just starting, you don't usually have the option of taking a writer to Acapulco – or even to Accrington. But should you try to entice a journalist to listen to your life story over a drink or three at the local boozer?

Maybe. Hacks who've had stuff poured down their throats and/or pushed up their noses have been known to become rather more, shall we say, receptive to their hosts' ideas. But in the cold light of next day, they may well revert to professional mode and scorn your pathetic attempts to ingratiate yourselves. If, however, some goodwill *already* exists, a little lubrication may well get the wheels turning a bit faster.

But do not, under any circumstances, expect journalists to be grateful for your hospitality. As far as they're concerned, they're doing you far more of a favour by giving you a little ear-time than you're doing by fronting them a couple of drinks.

And while we're on the subject, here are six other things not to do.

1   Don't get your dad to phone up and ask for a front cover on the basis that you look just like Paul McCartney.

2   Don't demand that a London music paper sends one of its writers to Glasgow to review your next pub gig unless *you're* paying.

3   Don't behave as if you have a right to be written about – you don't. Arrogance of this sort is a real turn-off – but so too is crawling. Steer a middle path.

4   Don't turn up at a music paper's offices unannounced and expect to be welcomed with open arms. People do have to work there. Phone first, and if nobody wants to meet you, be satisfied with dropping off your stuff at reception.

5   Don't turn up at a music paper dressed as a gorilla, a robot or a spaceman, in the belief that this stunt will direct desirable attention in your direction. It won't.

6   Don't imagine that you're entitled to an objective review – there is no such thing. Music journalists are paid to write *subjective opinions*. So if you want an assessment of your live show that reports the number of people in the audience, invite a statistician, not a music critic.

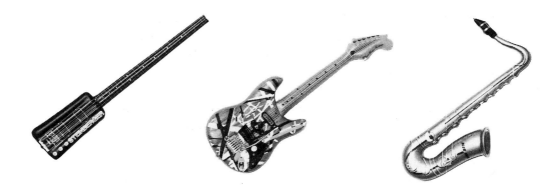

Freebies

Tee-shirts, fancy packaging and other gimmicks are often used as promotional accompaniments to singles or albums. Do they help you to get press?

If you do a good tee-shirt, sweatshirt or jacket, people will definitely wear it if it doesn't turn them into too obvious a walking advert for you. It may then add to your hipness quotient, but on its own, it's unlikely to get you any more column inches.

Any kind of cool-looking packaging always makes the contents seem more desirable; a good promo package can actually get your record listened to, where otherwise it would have been ignored. But if the record's junk, it'll still end up where all the rest of the junk ends up.

And other freebies? If they're useful, they'll be used. If they're decorative, they may be stuck on a wall or shelf somewhere. But they're only ever the icing on the cake, and if the cake is stale to begin with, don't waste your money.

Do promo freebies like these 'Blowhard' inflatables, t-shirts or posters get you press? Almost certainly not. But the punters like them, and music paper offices would be duller without them.

The Smash Hits
phenomenon

The traditional music press means the three tabloid weeklies: *NME* (music, politics, lifestyle), *Sounds* (rock, indies, instruments) and *Melody Maker* (musical mixed bag, instruments). But since the early '80s, all have been steadily losing ground to the glossy pop publications which sprung up to cater for the video generation, and their circulations, at between 50,000 and 100,000, are half what they were ten years ago.

Of the glossies, by far the biggest success story is *Smash Hits*. With a fortnightly circulation of over half a million and a readership of Bros-adoring teens and pre-teens, it is simultaneously reviled and respected throughout the business. Its influence upon this age group is akin to that of *Top Of The Pops* and the Saturday morning kids' TV shows (see *Radio and TV* chapter). So if that's your intended market, ignore it at your peril!

Other music
mags

Nearest competitor to *Smash Hits* is *Number One* with half the market-leader's sales. But on a weekly basis, it still beats the combined sales of the tabloid weeklies.

Other glossies to consider are the chart and dance-music orientated *RM* (*Record Mirror*) and the metal fans' bible *Kerrang!*, with sales of around 50,000 and 100,000 respectively.

Adult orientated rock? The monthly *Q* should be on your hit list.

Style before content? *The Face, Sky, Blitz* and *ID* (all monthly) are there to serve you.

Confirmed musos? There's a wide range of technical monthlies that carry interviews, including *Guitarist, Home & Studio Recording, International Musician & Recording World, Keyboard Player, Making Music, Music Technology,* and *Sound On Sound*.

Easy Street

The Fleet Street papers are, today, a prime target for those who wish to create a hit phenomenon without the millstone of having to get their talents first recognised by the music press. This is particularly useful to people whose talents might not stand up to close scrutiny, but who have something else to offer. Such as sheer, ruthless determination to get to the top at any price, preferably without doing anything to deserve it.

Fleet Street likes that, because Fleet Street is full of people like that.

Along with television, Fleet Street has created a new genre of contemporary music: careerist pop. Careerist pop is based on a keen sense of what's marketable: what to say, what to wear, which clubs to be seen in and which people to be seen with. It has nothing to do with talent, nothing to do with quality and very little to do with music — because the effort put into selling the image creates a chartwards momentum all of its own.

And it works: it sells records and it can make you a star. But you better get yourself a suit of armour while you're on the way up, because the knives'll be out for you on the way down. Play that game and you confirm your own disposability.

Meanwhile, here are ten ways careerist popsters can get coverage in the tabloid dailies:

1   Be the owner of very large breasts.

2   Give up sex, drugs and drink in favour of religion.

3   Give up religion in favour of sex, drugs and drink.

4 Admit that you are gay.

5 Admit that you are not gay.

6 Be a leggy blonde.

7 Know a story about Sean Penn and Madonna.

8 Make a guest appearance in a TV soap opera.

9 Turn down a guest appearance in a TV soap opera.

10 Get the cast of a TV soap opera to sing on your record.

11 Exaggerate everything.

The rest of the press

Pop and rock aren't just music business any more – they're everybody's business. And that means there are masses of publications apart from the tabloid dailies and the music press where your activities might be of interest. These include listings magazines, local papers, the daily and Sunday Fleet Street 'heavies', the weekend colour supplements, freebie commuter mags, the fashion press and a host of general interest publications.

Timing

Timing is very important in all matters relating to publicity. Many good ideas have failed because they've been offered for consumption at the wrong time; many bad ones have succeeded because the timing has been right. A sense of timing comes from having a good overall appreciation of what's happening in the business and in our culture as a whole. So keep your eyes and ears open, and when the time is right, go for it.

RADIO AND
TELEVISION

●▶●▶●▶ *Airplay's the game, old chap*

THE PRESS is important through the power of editorialising – people telling other people how good something or someone is – or isn't. The broadcast media essentially represent the other side of the coin: here, your work is simply *presented*, and the viewers and listeners either like it or they don't.

Of course repetition is a form of editorialising; radio and TV are not going to play the pants off a song they think is useless. But the real job is not in convincing the media of how good you are, more in convincing them how popular *they* will be by offering the likes of you to the public.

Whether it's state-run Aunty Beeb or a red hot commercial radio station, all are bound in one way or another by their paymasters' response: the BBC by its figures-watching producers and directors, the commercial companies by advertisers.

The vast majority of hit records are made so thanks to exposure on national radio and TV. Regular appearances on either (though one tends to follow the other) almost guarantees chart success. The competition to get on playlists, or to get a still highly coveted slot on *Top Of The Pops* is fierce and (in the past was for certain) riddled with foul play.

Naturally the media never admit to current skullduggery, and nor do they admit to their other major shortcoming: that of feeling they must pump out the least offensive, least demanding music they can in order to attract (they think) as large an audience as possible.

At time of writing, during the gestation of satellite and deregulated television, it's too early to know whether, as the optimists claim, wider *choice* will indeed mean wider choice, or just a larger number of people churning out the same stuff. But if American broadcasting is anything to go by, which it normally is, the signs are not exactly encouraging.

Manipulating the media, becoming a 'media person' is an art all in itself. And you're either born with it or must spend considerable time and effort constructing

John Peel, one of the 'Beeb's' longest-serving DJs and continued champion of the Indie scene.

your 'personality', complete with one or all of the following: memorably strange name (de rigueur for a TV figure whether natural or assumed, viz Bamber Gascoigne, Magnus Magnusson, Oprah Winfrey ...), striking haircut/glasses, crazy clothes and distinctive speaking voice.

Armed with the above, your music can be as dull and conventional as mud and you'll probably still get away with it.

The less media-*obsessive* route is knowing how to use the media as and when you need – being played on the right radio shows, sessions maybe, appearances on Saturday morning kids' TV etc – like when you have a record to promote.

The big thing here is co-ordination. A one-off TV appearance may boost your ego but unless it was a truly stunning performance or you start going berserk *à la Sex Pistols* with Bill Grundy (when the use of four letter words heralded the start of the band's career and the end of Grundy's), it won't be worth a row of beans without the benefit of radio play, a video being shown here and there etc.

Radio 1

Radio 1 is the nation's hitmaking radio station, whether anyone likes it or not. Other stations can, occasionally, break a record, and a club hit can cross over to mainstream success – though normally only after Radio 1 has been forced to pick up on it. But, exceptions to prove the rule aside, Radio 1 dictates the singles charts and, if you want a hit, you'd better make sure your record is being played on it.

Understanding what makes Radio 1 tick isn't the most inspiring discovery, but at least it may help figure out why your record is *not* being played and help you to focus your attention on a more likely candidate next time.

Radio 1's job is to entertain the nation with pop music; to keep the truck driver's spirits up as he battles through London traffic, to keep the girls on the assembly line from going crazy with boredom, to temper the noise of high speed drilling in the garage workshop, to break the ice in the hairdresser's. In other words, to provide music for working people while they work, to relieve some of the pressure of doing so.

If your music requires serious listening or a contemplative frame of mind to be appreciated, your chances of gaining a slot on the playlist are hopeless. Okay, so once in a while a record comes along that the DJs and producers can file under 'weepy' or 'something for the hip grannies', but for most of the time, what is wanted is FUN FUN FUN, with as many titles as possible with the word DANCE in them.

The playlist

The Radio 1 playlist is literally what it sounds like: a list of records that will be played a guaranteed number of times per week. The precise format may change from time to time but essentially, records are chosen by a small panel of BBC producers and put into a number of categories: No; the odd play; quite a few plays; play it to death.

Records frequently move about through these categories (though it'll take quite a dance hit or massive listener demand to revive a 'No' vote); most records by little known artists start off in a lower 'rotation' so the producers can watch and wait. Only major artists like Michael Jackson or George Michael can expect to land an 'A' listing from release date.

Playlists are selected by producers, not DJs. DJs do make some of their own choices but the producers are the ones in charge. It is them you need to convince. It is to them that pluggers plug.

No one knows exactly what it takes to convince a BBC producer that your record has major hit potential because no such formula exists. The two most positive suggestions are: make lively, thrashy, trashy pop records as do, currently, Stock Aitken Waterman or in the past, Chinn/Chapman or Mickie Most, and then hire the best plugger in the business.

In the evenings Radio 1 dons its 'serious pop music' hat. Accordingly – and because the bulk of its audience is now at home and if it's the last thing they want to do it's listen to any more radio – the audience figures, playlist influence, and power to make a hit are all considerably reduced.

Nightime Radio 1 is important though, especially when it's catering to specialist music areas like metal, soul and dancefloor. Producers of the specialist programmes will almost certainly be more approachable, even if the competition to appear (on a John Peel session for instance) remains as fierce as always.

Local radio

Can plays on local radio get you a hit? In a word, no. Occasionally a major station like Capital in London or BRMB in Birmingham can do a pretty effective job, but in any such case where a record has 'broken out' of a local station, the artist probably had a massive local following to begin with.

Local radio stations, whether independent or BBC, tend to ape Radio 1 in their pop coverage. They have little choice. Advertisers on independent stations want the audience figures and the audiences want to hear hits – new or old.On the other hand, local BBC stations seem content to do their 'local' bit with news and human interest programmes, leaving the music programming very much along the lines of Radios 1 and 2, depending upon the schedule.

But local stations are still important because the competition to be interviewed, or to do special sessions for them, is minimal compared with national radio.

Pat Sharpe and Mick Browne present the Network charts on Capital Radio, supplied by MRIB and generally reckoned to be a more accurate and speedier reflection of public mood than the BBC's Gallup chart.

Local radio tours need to be organised, and co-ordinated with all other media efforts. Getting stations to agree to interview you (especially if you're playing locally, or have some local connection) is not difficult. Normally they're only too pleased to have something 'different' to offer the listeners.

A typical approach would be from your manager to the station controller or a likely (ie pop music orientated) DJ. A phone call followed by a record plus info followed by a phone call should suffice.

How much such activities will help you produce a hit depends on how thoroughly you do the rounds and how good you are at being interviewed or playing 'live' on radio.

Good radio interviews are upbeat, zany, provocative without being offensive, and fun. Serious comes across as miserable. Miserable as catatonic.

The questions you'll be asked are invariably:

• • • • • • • ➤ How long have you been together?
• • • • • • • ➤ How did you choose your name?
• • • • • • • ➤ How do you like (wherever you are)?
• • • • • • • ➤ Where are you playing tonight?
• • • • • • • ➤ What can you tell us about your record?

Prepare some suitably entertaining answers and remember that you can use the same stories over and over again as you move around the country. You may have heard yourself say the same thing a million times but in each area *they'll* be hearing it for the first time.

Television

Although the power of television cannot be underestimated, few artists owe their first hit to a TV appearance, more the other way around. TV simply pushes a record that's already bubbling somewhere into the mainstream of national awareness.

Top Of The Pops (BBC1)

Although it has more rivals than its radio equivalent, *Top Of The Pops* is the Radio 1 of pop television. Analysed, it's an abysmally low budget, tacky, mindless heap of junk, with vapid commentaries and wonky sets. But it's always been like that and it has been a rip-roaring success for more than 20 years, to the point where an appearance on the programme has come to be viewed as the very embodiment of hit status. Indeed to the public, if it wasn't on *TOTP*, it wasn't a hit.

No other pop TV show is worse than *Top Of The Pops*; all, no matter how under-funded, manage to look more interesting, cover more stimulating bands, have interviews, better camera angles ... but none have that aura of hitdom surrounding them and none are more difficult to get onto.

To get on *Top Of The Pops* you need a chart placing. Precisely where varies, and of course there are always stories about this band or that who seemed to appear out of nowhere. By and large though, you are guaranteed some sort of showing on the programme once your record is poised to become a hit. Unless you turn in a really shambolic performance, most records should zoom up the charts the week following an appearance.

Specialist pop shows

The turnover of other pop-based TV shows is fast; the shows being almost as transitory as the industry they feed on. From time to time, programmes aiming at and for the younger musician appear, but most stick pretty closely to well-known or chart artists for the simple reason that they've got advertisers breathing down their necks.

Getting you a slot on most pop TV shows is a job for professionals. Ringing up the producer yourself is unlikely to meet with much success. There again, the worst they can say is 'bugger off' so you've got nothing to lose.

Though no other show equals the power of *TOTP*, *any* specialist pop show is worth appearing on. And if you make it, don't blow it. Get advice, dancers, stylists, choreographers, whatever it takes.

Kids'/general entertainment shows

Saturday morning kids' shows are highly contested platforms for young bands to appear on.

Not only do their large and highly impressionable (they'll buy what they see) audiences watch on a purely musical level, but the programmes are prime breeding grounds for tomorrow's teen idols since most afford time for artists to speak and do phone-ins, and so offer them the chance to transform themselves from boring nobodies into worshipped heroes in the space of about five minutes.

A slot on a general entertainment show hosted, normally, by some buck-toothed comedian or ageing crooner, is a slot to be wary of unless you're looking for hit on the granny ticket. Fortunately, such shows are as likely to want you if you're an unknown pop band as you are to need them.

Talent shows

On the other hand this type of show might want you. With very few exceptions an appearance or, God forbid, a win, on one of these is likely to be the kiss of death to your career and definitely the kiss of death to your credibility. Only enter if you are looking for a hit in order to play the cabaret circuit on the back of it (if you're lucky) for the rest of your days.

The charts

If Top Of The Pops confers hit status, it does so because of its slavish devotion to the definition of a hit, that of being featured in the higher regions of the national pop charts.

Nowadays there are charts for this and that – Indie charts, Soul charts, Metal charts etc – but there are only two of any real importance in the UK: the MRIB Network Chart and the Gallup Chart.

Currently *Top Of The Pops* and Radio 1 take their cue from Gallup, a company that has a network of some 500 shops around the country (Chart Return shops) which are armed with special computers for logging the catalogue number of every record sold.

To safeguard against that age-old business of chart-rigging, if a record by an unknown artist were suddenly to sell hundreds of copies in a couple of particular chart return shops (and every record company knows which ones they are), some form of investigation would be mounted to see if the record had ever sold anywhere else.

All well and good, but record sales are not what they were. If you were to plot a route around the country's chart return shops buying up, say, just *one* copy of your record in each, a) no-one would ever get suspicious, and b) it would enter the Top 50.

Fiddling of one sort or another is impossible to stamp out. Few if any chart return shops pay for their records, and all are constantly festooned with picture disks, special sleeves and other promotional paraphernalia. In a strange way, it is this situation which is Gallup's best protection, since it's not the selling of the

Individual radio stations can have an impact in specialist areas. Pirates' Kiss FM (now bidding for a legit franchise) broke the club-related sampler-based dance music that finally crossed over into the mainstream charts.

records *from* the stores that's the problem, but getting the wretched things *into* the stores in the first place.

Unless you're prepared to fiddle on a massive scale – buying up hundreds of actual records over a period of weeks as well as buying up 'numbers' in the computer – fiddling is not going to get you into the Top 20. At some stage, genuine sales must start to take off. But once you're in the lower regions of the charts, things can begin to build of their own accord.

Playlisting is very much chart based, so you'll have muscle there. Influential magazines may hold out until you reach the Top 50 before covering you in depth with a special photo session etc. Once you get high enough, *Top Of The Pops* will have to acknowledge your existence.

The MRIB chart, as favoured by the *Network Chart Show* (ITV), Capital Radio, and many national newspapers, is generally reckoned to be a more accurate and speedier reflection of the public's mood, and less liable to fiddling – two reasons why its popularity with the powers that be is somewhat lukewarm.

The reason is that this chart is not just sales based. A panel of expert observers take into account sales, radio play, whether an artist is playing live . . . and then base the chart placings accordingly.

The reason it is less fiddleable is that should, using the earlier example, you tootle around the country buying up your own records and a) not have been heard of before, b) not be getting any radio play, c) not have your record being played in the clubs or d) not be playing live at the moment, MRIB won't just *think* it's a fiddle – it'll be a fiddle for certain!

CHAPTER
SIXTEEN

PLAYING LIVE

•➤•➤•➤ *One-thousand-and-one one-nighters*

YOU'LL know if playing live is going to help you make a hit record because you'll *be* playing live, you'll be loving it, and you'll be popular.

Today, when videos, mimed TV appearances and general hype combine to the extent that an ability to perform your music *at all* represents only one of many possible skills needed for record success, braving the various worlds of theatres, roadies, rehearsals, lighting rigs, feedback, monitors and the general public cannot be recommended lightly.

Playing live is a route to record success only if your live appearances

Support tours are a minefield. Prince, seen here with dancer Cat, may be a megastar now, but was massacred when he supported the Stones in America – and that was *after* he had hit records.

transcend (or *might* transcend) your recorded performances. Examples range from Alice Cooper whose snakework could hardly have been captured on vinyl, and Gary Glitter with his ridiculous costumes and chants, to major touring bands who've turned The Rock Concert into a form of religious festivity – like the Grateful Dead, ZZ Top and U2 – to artists who simply put on a spectacular show, like Prince, Tina Turner and of course Michael Jackson.

The theory behind playing live (and one that certainly explains the customary mad scramble for the exit at the end) is that having seen you, the public cannot wait to rush out and buy your latest release.

Fine if you've acquitted yourself well. In reality many concerts, in which ticket prices and T-shirts receive more attention than sound quality and stagecraft, serve only to piss the audience off, fleecing them of their last buck in the process so they can't afford to buy the record *anyway*.

In America, The Home of Rock 'n' Roll, things are different: from spontaneous combustions down at the local bar, to happy-hour three-pieces at the Holiday Inn, to college prom nights, to stadia-hopping megastar 'events', live music has a magic that records can never hope to match.

In seen-it-all-before, cynical England, for live music to help sell records, it

In Britain, playing live is not a route to hit records unless your performance on stage transcends your performance in the studio. Michael Jackson is an artist who amazes with both.

must do something else; perhaps involve the type of 'fuck you' violence associated with punk, perhaps the tribal mania of metal, or just the sheer can't-knock-it showmanship of a Michael Jackson.

What it boils down to is this: at the end of the 1980s, playing live has become a luxury; live music venues are evaporating every week and, rather as it always has at anything other than pub gig or Wembley Stadium levels, it'll *cost* the artist to perform.

This is the situation in 1989 anyhow. Whether new forms of music and/or entertainment will rise up to a) revive live music or b) complete its assassination is anyone's guess.

But in spite of this grantedly gloomy outlook, people do continue to perform. Is it worth it, if so at what level, what can you hope to get out of it, and how can you maximise the returns from your efforts?

Answers differ depending on whether you're starting off your career in music or whether you're already making records but not, as yet, hit ones.

America breeds live acts of Bruce Springsteen's calibre because at every level, from local bar jam to stadium rock event, live music in the USA still has a magic that records can never match.

The value of playing live in order to get a record deal

Obvious in a way. If you're good, people will soon get to hear about you; eventually, therefore, including a person from a record company.

There's no point in rationalising why people form bands and start playing. You do it because you want to. Nowadays, the more interesting study is the case *against* forming a band or playing live, covered, to some extent, in the home studio and press sections.

But you might be a borderline case: someone who's got musical ability but no 'live' experience; demos aplenty but no stagecraft.

The plus points of joining or forming a band in this instance can include the chance to:

●●●●●●●◗ See how the public reacts to your music
●●●●●●●◗ Improve your playing ability
●●●●●●●◗ Gather raw material for songs
●●●●●●●◗ Interact with other musicians
●●●●●●●◗ Pay your dues
●●●●●●●◗ Earn money at music (see above)
●●●●●●●◗ Get discovered

On the other hand, playing live could:

●●●●●●●◗ Diffuse your focus away from making a hit record
●●●●●●●◗ Be too time/energy consuming
●●●●●●●◗ Be too much hassle
●●●●●●●◗ Be an unnecessary strain on personal relationships

In a practical sense, playing live is going to help a record company make its mind up about you. Demos are all well and good. But did you do all the playing, how long did it take, did the engineer come up with all those great lines? Many such doubts can be dispelled from A&R minds by seeing you play.

Seeing you live will also add another dimension to your appeal; a scout who's got to convince an entire department of your hit potential is well armed if he can say, 'The demo's great but wait 'til you see them live.'

On a more subtle level, when you're negotiating with a record company, to have the draw of gigs, as in 'we're playing at so and so tonight if you want to come', should keep interested parties interested until the deal is done.

Finally, never mind about technology and all that – you'll find that few record companies like dealing with artists who can't perform, especially if you purport to be a group. It's just not quite rock 'n' roll.

Showcases

It probably won't come down to this but it may. A showcase gig can be either a proper gig set up by your manager in order to 'show' you off to prospective record companies. Or it can be like an audition, where you play on stage – normally in a large rehearsal/showcase facility – to personnel from a record company only.

The first scenario isn't wonderful but it's okay. Relax, don't treat it too seriously, just play and perform as well as you can. The second, if you're not used to auditioning, can be a nightmare.

But it needn't be. The chances are the record company people will be only marginally less embarrassed or ill-at-ease than you. So just pretend that it's a normal, regular gig. Then so can they. Tell yourself there's a vast, screaming audience out there and perform.

The support tour

Having signed a record deal and having made a record, the next pressure you'll come under will be the support tour. Pressure may be from yourselves, it may be from your management, certainly from your agent, or possibly from all sides, record company included.

Be very careful.

Support tours (opening the show for a major act) can, at best, be a rather expensive way to learn the ropes of touring and playing on large stages. At worst they can be a total waste of time and money – *your* time and money – and can even harm your career.

You won't often hear this advice for the simple reason that the support tour supports too many people within the industry. Too many people (though not you) have too much to gain.

Agents love them for obvious reasons. You're playing, they'll take a cut – a little now but hopefully more in the future. Managements love them because they get you out of their hair ('put 'em on a support tour for Chrissakes'), promoters love them because someone's got to open the show for the headliners, headline acts love them because they help underwrite a tour (most charge a buy-on fee). And record companies tolerate them – even though they're the ones who'll have to stump up the buy-on plus fund your own running costs – because they buy them time.

Time for your record to chart *anyway*, time for their own publicity machine to grind into action, time for them to assess what to do with you next.

And at the end of the day, you'll love (the idea of) them because you'll be

Scottish band Simple Minds reached their world class status by gigging solidly for years, building up the kind of grass roots following that would eventually guarantee massive record sales.

getting the chance to play in front of large audiences/have a road crew/go to America/play with your heroes . . . whatever it takes.

What you may not have reckoned with is this: Instead of playing in front of large audiences, you're more likely to be playing in front of small audiences at large venues. The problem is that you'll be playing as the punters are coming in, or worse, waiting to.

You'll only be given a fraction of the headliner's lights and PA to work with. The amounts vary depending upon how decent (or daft) the act, but there's no way you'll be booming out at full blast in a blaze of glory.

Headline acts with diehard fans will hate you. Boos and bottles are quite common (Prince was massacred in America supporting the Stones on their tour – and that was *after* he'd had hit records!).

Touring expenses will be vast (you'll have to cover distances and times that may be financially viable for the headline act but will be murderous for you, eg Amsterdam on Monday; three days off while headliner does telly; then Brussels on Thursday) and all you'll have coming in will be the nominal sum 'paid' to you each night.

If, in spite of the above, you manage to convince anything more than scattered pockets of the headliner's audience that *your* record is worth buying too, the

The 'magic' number of beats per minute to guarantee you'll get 'em on the dancefloor is supposedly 120, But Chic's all-time-classic dance hit 'Le Freak' broke that rule with a BPM of 122.

group will more than likely kick you off the tour. Your job is to be good. But not *that* good. Encores, for instance, are cardinal sins.

For every act that crossed over into stardom thanks to a support tour, there's a thousand that didn't and another thousand that won't. Support tours, if undertaken at all, should be undertaken once only.

To gain a reputation for being a good support act (you don't complain, you're good but not a threat and have a nice road crew), or worse, to become *sought after* as such, does not make for a hit career.

However, if you still cannot resist it:

- Don't choose to support a Big Name on the way down; better a middle one on the way further up.
- Don't get talked into supporting your management's Other Act (you'll always be playing second fiddle in their eyes, whereas with an unrelated act, at least you'll be your management's priority).
- Observe the main act every night. Learn why they're there and you're here.
- Act like stars. Don't get pushed around.
- ONLY DO IT ONCE.

Club tours

You may play to as many people in a week of club tours as the hall holds on one night of a support tour, but at least the audience will be yours. Well, not shared with someone else at any rate.

People will also think of you differently. On a club tour, if you're seen and liked, the chances are people will remember your name, as in 'I saw this great band, the ***** last night down at *****'. Whereas on a support tour, it's more like 'great support act – I can't remember who they were'.

This said, a British club tour must rank as one of the most depressing undertakings known to man. If you can survive it, you really do deserve a hit record. The question is, will it help you get one?

It will if you can talk yourself into if not enjoying it, then at least recognising its purpose.

Unless you're going to fiddle your entire way into the charts, you will need a groundswell of support from devoted fans who'll buy your every release regardless. This is how you find such support. At gigs where you can see faces and talk to people afterwards, before the day comes when you're surrounded by minders.

Combined, as every-good club tour should be, with copious radio appearances and appearances at the hipper dance clubs, this enables you to begin carving out

Whitney Houston, like Tina Turner, is one of a still relatively small number of female superstars who are as highly regarded for their live work as for their records.

a loyal hardcore of fans on which your your first hit will depend – just to get the ball rolling.

University tours

The first thing to realise about college and university tours is that students don't have any money. Even if they love you, they're broke, and are far more likely to tape your record than buy it.

So what's the point in doing these tours?

In the quest for hit records, not a lot. But such tours can make you money (the students themselves may be broke but the social secs/events officers [wot run these things] still have considerable amounts of money to blow on bands. And they can give you credibility, which will convert into sales once your student audience has left college and got jobs which pay enough for them to buy your records and go to your gigs. Provided you're still around by then.

The last word

As a postscript to this chapter, there are of course many other considerations to deal with when playing live: road crew, equipment, truck hire, accommodation, none of which have any direct bearing on whether your records become hits or not, but all of which have a very direct bearing on how painful or pleasurable – and profitable – the process will have been.

Although there is a relation between playing live and selling records, it's not as automatic as you might think.

In the past, artists who have been (rightly) famed for their prowess live – such as Zappa, Grateful Dead, the Stones even – have not, in the first two cases especially, sold that many records. Similarly of course, pop history is littered with one-hit wonders who lost their pants on subsequent overblown world tours.

You've got to earn popularity as a live act by being good at it. A string of hit singles doesn't automatically give you the right to Wembley Stadium.

PICTURE CREDITS

INDEX